Karl Albrecht is a management consultant, lecturer, and instructor at the University of California extension, San Diego. He works with business executives and professionals to increase effectiveness through teamwork, effective problem solving, and innovation.

KARL ALBRECHT

EXECUTIVE TUNE-UP

PERSONAL EFFECTIVENESS SKILLS FOR BUSINESS AND PROFESSIONAL PEOPLE

A SPECTRUM BOOK

PRENTICE-HALL, INC., Englewood Cliffs, New Jersey 07632

Library of Congress Cataloging in Publication Data

Albrecht, Karl A.
   Executive tune-up.

   (A Spectrum Book)
   Includes index.
   1. Executives.   2. Self-actualization (Psychology).
3. Interpersonal relations.   4. Industrial sociology.
I. Title.
HF5500.2.A424   658.4'093   80–25686
ISBN 0–13–294215–1
ISBN 0–13–294207–0 (pbk.)

Editorial/production supervision
  and interior design by Heath Lynn Silberfeld
Cover © 1981 Judith Kazdym Leeds
Manufacturing buyer: Barbara A. Frick

© 1981 by Prentice-Hall, Inc., Englewood Cliffs, New Jersey 07632
Photos (pages 36, 86, 95, and 163) © 1981 by Karl Albrecht

A SPECTRUM BOOK

10 9 8 7 6 5 4 3 2 1

Printed in the United States of America

Prentice-Hall International, Inc., London
Prentice-Hall of Australia Pty. Limited, Sydney
Prentice-Hall of Canada, Ltd., Toronto
Prentice-Hall of India Private Limited, New Delhi
Prentice-Hall of Japan, Inc., Tokyo
Prentice-Hall of Southeast Asia Pte. Ltd., Singapore
Whitehall Books Limited, Wellington, New Zealand

CONTENTS

8
PRACTICAL ACTION 70

9
MANAGING STRESS
AND DEVELOPING WELLNESS 84

III
SOCIAL COMPETENCE:
GETTING ALONG
WITH OTHERS

10
DEVELOPING AN EFFECTIVE
INTERPERSONAL STYLE 104

11
COMMUNICATING ADAPTIVELY 115

16
DEVELOPING YOUR
MANAGEMENT SKILLS 170

do you want a management job? 171, the "new manager"
syndrome 172, four dimensions of managerial
competence 173, assessing your managerial skills 174

17
MANAGING A GROUP
OF PEOPLE EFFECTIVELY 176

enabling people vs. commanding them 177, a model of
leadership style 178, managing by objectives 179,
building a team 180, handling controversy and
conflict 180, allocating your time and energy
effectively 181

V
GETTING ALONG
IN ORGANIZATIONS

18
UNDERSTANDING
ORGANIZATIONAL
POLITICS 184

an organization as a social system 185, the chain of
command 186, positive politics: getting ahead with your
values intact 187, p.o.w.e.r.: who has it? 189, creating
your political "molecule" 190, managing your boss 192,
rules for political success 192

19
SPECIAL PROBLEMS
OF WOMEN IN ORGANIZATIONS 194

women's mobility 195, the "ole boy" network 196, the "ole
girl" network 197, some useful strategies for upwardly
mobile women 199

PREFACE

Sooner or later most business and professional people reach a turning point in mid-career—a "stop-and-think" stage at which they begin to take stock, think back over their lives and careers, and reflect seriously on the future. They wonder about their achievements, their expectations, their basic values, the rewards they get from their current situations, and their possibilities for the future. Many of them also take a renewed interest in their health at this stage, realizing the fundamental part it will play in the enjoyment of the rest of their lives. They usually find they need a "tune-up."

A person who comes to this critical stage usually feels a need for some kind of framework for the review process. It helps to have a well-organized structure or a model of some kind which will help a person go about the process logically and somewhat systematically.

This book provides such a framework. If you put to use the concepts and methods offered here, you can reasonably expect to:

1. Gain a clearer understanding of yourself as a person—your values, your purposes, your major desires, your needs for development, and the choices open to you about what to do with the rest of your life.

2. Establish a sense of firm control over your life; develop an attitude and a capability for self-management which puts you squarely in charge of your life and your career, and which enables you to make your choices according to your own values.

3. Focus your energies more effectively to get the results you want in your life; clarify your values, set goals, make

plans, organize your activities, and manage your time to get the important things done and eliminate distracting influences which tend to pull you away from your main purposes.

4. Keep your emotions on an even keel; consciously manage your mood, keep your stress level within the healthy "comfort zone," and maintain a highly positive frame of mind virtually all the time, even in the face of the negativism that prevails in so much of our society.

5. Eliminate from your life negative or counterproductive influences; clarify and improve your relationships with others, and keep them positive.

6. Manage your entire life pattern, including your fitness and health habits, to feel good, stay healthy, and maximize the quality of your life.

7. Become fully self-renewing; keep your life active, productive, stimulating, and interesting.

This book provides a comprehensive framework for thinking about *personal effectiveness* and for developing the specific skills that comprise it. This framework, or "competence model," describes and analyzes the primary dimensions of personal effectiveness in terms of *Mood Control* skills, *Self-Actualization* skills, *Practical Action* skills, and *Social* skills. These four "macro-skills," or broad categories of competence, taken together form the basis for your total effectiveness in life, relationships, and career. Note that this book focuses on *skills* and *actions* in describing personal effectiveness. Rather than dwell upon emotion for its own sake, or toss about the empty metaphors of "growth," which R.D. Rosen has so aptly named "psychobabble," this book proceeds from the premise that effectiveness in anything amounts to the ability to get certain results. A desired result implies the need for successful action. Successful action implies the need for competence. Hence we begin with the matter of competence in analyzing and developing personal effectiveness.

For example, you can keep your frame of mind highly positive, and consequently keep yourself on an even keel emotionally, by developing the specific skills of *Mood Control*. These amount to consciously developed psychomotor skills, coupled with techniques such as positive attention, input selection, and positive "self-talk."

Self-Actualization skills include clarifying values, identifying priorities, and making choices in your life. *Practical-Action* skills include personal problem solving, setting goals, making plans, getting organized, and managing your time. *Social* skills include the actions you take to get what you want in dealing with other people while maintaining positive relationships and good will with them.

This book treats these skills from several points of view. First, we have the focus on you as an individual. This deals with your sense of your own authority and power in your life, your self-esteem, your values, and your choices. Next come interactions you have with other people on a one-to-one basis. These skills then become useful, along with others, in dealing with other people in group situations, such as at work. And finally we have the level of the organization, in which many business and professional people work.

The book also helps you to think through your career and to consider carefully the matter of "getting into management." It provides a look at the managerial job and shows what skills you will need to handle it. It also helps you think through your "political" relationships with others in the organization and to determine what you need to do to get ahead while keeping your personal value system intact.

And most importantly, we deal with personal effectiveness as a matter of *balanced reward*—the policy of maximizing the "return on investment" from each of the major dimensions of life you establish as important. By investing your energies strategically and in a balanced way, you can enjoy a sense of satisfaction in each of these areas. This makes you a self-actualizing, motivated, self-managing individual, living effectively and happily, because you understand and acknowledge your role as the "chief executive" in your life.

BASIC CONCEPTS OF PERSONAL EFFECTIVENESS

1

INTRODUCTION

effectiveness and ineffectiveness

Your effectiveness in any life situation or life role begins with your effectiveness *as a person*. You can function effectively as a husband, wife, lover, manager, stockbroker, musician, salesperson, student, secretary, father, mother, neighbor, or friend, to the extent that you possess certain basic competencies which transcend all of these roles. This book proposes a framework for studying human competence on this transcendent level — the level of basic human functional skills which enable you to live effectively, in fulfillment of your own needs and values.

What constitutes "personal effectiveness"? What, for that matter, constitutes "ineffectiveness"? How do we know when we have either one, and to what extent? Why does one person seem to enjoy life so fully — experiencing, learning, and growing — while another seems frustrated, unhappy, unfulfilled, and immobilized? How does one person get most of what he or she wants out of life, while another manages to make a shambles out of it? Why do many Americans have more money, more material possessions, and more free time than ever before, and yet express so much dissatisfaction with their lives? Why do some people figuratively beat their heads against imaginary walls of their own construction, unable to take charge of their own lives?

We *can* find answers to these questions — explicit, understandable answers which suggest practical action and problem solving. We can indeed *define* personal effectiveness and its counterpart, ineffectiveness. Underlying the tremendous diversity of human experience and human behavior, we can discern certain styles of action which make the difference. The mosaic of ordinary human misery, inefficiency, and ineffectiveness has a definite pattern, which we can decode and understand. And we can create an alternative mosaic — a pattern of ideas, attitudes, and actions, which we can call general human competence.

The essential difference between effectiveness and ineffectiveness, which we will explore thoroughly in this book, lies in one key point: the acceptance of the fact that what you do has a cause-and-effect relationship to what happens to you. We will define personal effectiveness as a specific set of *skills in action*, explicitly rejecting much of the contemporary "self-help" viewpoint which preoccupies itself with emotion for its own sake and which flounders about in a verbal quagmire of terms like "growing," "getting it together," "getting in touch with your feelings," and "being yourself." I propose a highly operational definition of effectiveness, based on *doing* whatever you need to do to accomplish your ends and actualize your most important values.

Most people use the term *happiness* in evaluating their lives and their circumstances, and we can use it in our explorations as well. Presumably, one's level of happiness serves as a sort of barometer of the quality of his life. When one feels happy in general, he deduces that "life is going well." When he feels generally unhappy, he takes this as evidence of something wrong with whatever he considers his "life." The crucial difference between the highly effective individual and the chronically ineffective one lies in their respective attitudes about the causes of happiness and unhappiness. The ineffective person usually believes that happiness or unhappiness more or less happens to him. The effective person realizes that he becomes happy as a result of what he does. This entire book rests upon the thesis that you don't *have* happiness — you *do* happiness.

you probably need a "tune-up"

As an adult, professional, working person, you may have reached a point in your life and your career where you've achieved many of the most basic things you wanted when you left home and struck out on your own. Probably, you learned how to get a job, make a steady income, get ahead at a reasonable pace in your job, manage your money, save up for many of the things you wanted, and establish a household. Perhaps you also learned to raise children and manage a family. In a general sense, you've "made it." At this point, you might want to look back and compare your present status with your original aspirations.

For most people, this comparison brings some mixed feelings. You might feel well satisfied with your mastery of the basic logistics of living, yet not entirely pleased with some of the other aspects. You might realize you haven't set any new goals recently, and your life may have drifted into a pattern of routine activity, with fewer and fewer occasions for doing something exciting or new and different, or for learning something new. You might have inadvertently drifted into the "activity trap" — a life situation analogous to the situation in a company setting, where people work energetically at various repetitive activities, yet can't clearly spell out their overall purposes.

If your life has followed a trajectory similar to that of a large majority of American professional people, you might also find yourself overweight and a bit out of shape. You might feel somewhat dissatisfied with your health habits, such as smoking, drinking, and overeating. If past thirty, you might recently have heard yourself commenting with an air of quiet resignation about "getting old." You might feel "basically OK," but lack that spark of energy and enthusiasm you had when you finished high school or college.

In your more reflective moments, perhaps you evaluate your overall life situation as basically fortunate, yet lacking a spark of excitement and newness. You might find that some of your key relationships have drifted into patterned, routine modes of interaction, with less enjoyment than you might like. If married, you might find your marriage less than rewarding, or possibly even problematical in itself. Perhaps other aspects of your life invite your attention.

Of course, you might judge that none of these trends holds true for your life. You might decide that your life provides everything you could ever probably want — in which case you've just finished reading this book. But if your experiences parallel mine and those of many of our professional colleagues, you probably want some newness, some excitement, some enrichment, possibly some problem solving, and some self-renewal.

You probably need a "tune-up." Just as an automobile occasionally needs a thorough going over to put it back into good running condition, you — and your body — could probably use a midcareer tune-up. By the word *tune-up* in this case, we mean an honest and constructive assessment, some decisions about what to change or add or eliminate in your life situation, and possibly the conscious development of some useful skills of personal effectiveness.

We might say that the first twenty-five years of a typical person's life happen more or less by accident, but after about that point he bears the responsibility for all the rest of life. For most of us midcareer presents a demand — and an opportunity — to rechart our personal courses and to define the life-styles we really want.

This book serves as a tune-up manual. It offers a way of defining personal effectiveness in terms of operational human skills; it offers some important concepts for thinking about one's self, one's life, and one's career; and it offers some specific techniques for acquiring and using these skills.

THE BEHAVIORAL APPROACH TO PERSONAL EFFECTIVENESS

a new language
for personal effectiveness

In discussing and analyzing personal effectiveness, I propose to use a very distinctive vocabulary and a very specific mode of description. I propose to use terms that describe *action*, as opposed to the currently popular vocabulary of terms that describe "being," "feeling," and "experiencing." I propose an operational definition of personal effectiveness as something you *do*, rather than something you have or experience. Adopting this point of view, we can consider all of the customary features of "happiness" as *results* of our actions, not as accidental or temporary conditions which exist in our lives as a matter of good fortune. Indeed, it makes much more sense to speak of "doing" happiness rather than having it. Instead of saying "I am happy," one should really say "I happied very well today."

Let's explore some of the ramifications of this shift in vocabulary. For example, we don't know how to help someone "get his head together," but we can show him how to *analyze* his life's problems, *identify* and *evaluate alternatives* for solving them, *make decisions* effectively, *make plans*, put his decisions into *action*, and *accept responsibility* for the results. If the results make him happier than before, then we've shown him how to function more effectively.

Similarly, we can't show someone how to "get in touch with his feelings," but we can show him how to *describe* the situation he reacted to, *identify* the signals in the situation to which he responded robotically, *verbalize* what he wanted to do at the instant of reaction, *acknowledge* his emotional response, and *decide* how to proceed in the situation.

Note the use of action verbs in these examples. Although some of these terms present more of a challenge for objective observation than others, they all have the common feature of explicitly describing the elements of the situation and the elements of action necessary to get the best from it under the circumstances.

Let's consider happiness, or whatever other term you'd like to use in assessing the quality of your life in all of its dimensions, to mean *the consequences of effective action*. We will take the quality of life as our barometer of the effectiveness with which we do what we do. If you can spell out the conditions in each key area of your life that you will consider objective measures of quality, then you can identify the actions you need to take and the skills you need to improve in order to create those conditions. Your professional life, your job and career, your private life, your friendships and working relationships with others, and your close personal relationships with a chosen few, all depend in a very significant way on what you do. You and I make our lives and careers happy or unhappy, depending on what we do. Let's accept that responsibility and get to work.

To carry out our task effectively, we need to get a firm grasp on the skill of *behavior description*. This refers to the practice of talking about what goes on between one's self and others in objective, action-oriented terms. Although you needn't change your entire language pattern in this way, nevertheless you will find that analyzing problematical situations and deciding what to do about them comes much easier if you can express them in concrete terms.

For example, you might replace the statement "I'm unhappy with my job" with more definitive statements like "I want to earn more money," "I want more responsibility," or "I want more recognition and reward for my accomplishments." The term "I want" will qualify as a form of behavior for our purposes, even though another person really couldn't observe it in the strictest sense. It gives you an idea of how to act on your discontent.

Similarly, you can apply the behavior description technique to clarify problem situations such as those involving close emotional relationships. You could revise the statement "He/she doesn't respect my feelings" and describe the specific things the other person did or didn't do to warrant that conclusion. Typical behaviors you might notice could include ridiculing you, criticizing you for feeling a certain way, speaking disparagingly of your values or beliefs, or breaking important promises.

Many so-called personality conflicts on the job continue for long periods because the protagonists don't recognize the impact of their individual behavior on each other, and often can't analyze the situation in behavioral terms. Terms of condemnation and accusation fly back and forth, such as "uncooperative," "inconsiderate," "narrow-minded," and "stupid," getting in the way of problem solving and adaptation. Countless people in countless organizations get fired or parked in dead-end jobs because of vaguely defined "attitude problems." The manager who can see beyond derogatory adjectives like "lazy," "unmotivated," "incompetent," and "uncooperative" and can identify the difference between the way the problem employee *behaves* and how he should behave for effective work performance, has a head start in getting the performance problem solved.

To practice and develop this skill of behavior description, watch carefully what goes on around you during a full day and see how many difficult or problematical situations you can find to analyze. Describe to yourself the key behaviors on the part of each of the participants, using fairly concrete and verifiable verbs. Identify specific behaviors on the part of any of the parties which might contribute to making the situation more difficult to resolve, and identify those you consider helpful or facilitative. In describing various situations and human events to others, increase the number of behavior-descriptive terms you use and note their reactions to the information. And in particular, get into the habit of describing your own behavior to yourself and to others in concrete, action-oriented terms.

three levels
of human development

Three descriptive categories can help us in thinking about human capability as a matter of developing useful competencies for living. We can identify, analyze, and evaluate various actions associated with these three levels of human development:

1. The *amoebic* level — the person who merely drifts with his circumstances. He responds to problems as they present themselves, he meets the basic requirements of living, goes to work, pays his taxes, does his shopping, eats his meals, watches television, goes to bed, and gets up the next day to repeat the process. Thoreau probably described about seventy-five percent of humanity with his famous statement, "The mass of men lead lives of quiet desperation."

2. The *cybernetic* level — the achievement-oriented, goal-striving person. He enjoys a much greater sense of personal satisfaction than the level-one person because he takes action to achieve specific results and reach specific goals. This person has some definite ideas of what he wants from life, and generally has a program of sorts for getting it. He has succeeded rather well in actualizing the primary values of his surrounding culture, which, in the United States, tend heavily toward financial wealth, material possessions, and the social status conferred by having them.

3. The *meta-cybernetic* level — the goal-oriented person who to a great extent defines his own values and purposes, with much less influence from the prevailing norms of the culture that surrounds him. He has a high level of what Abraham Maslow called "resistance to enculturation." He has liberated himself from inordinate obedience to the level-one and level-two values of conformity, approval of others, social status, and obedience to institutional status quo, and has managed to come to terms successfully with those around him who operate from levels one and two.

We will use level three, the *meta-cybernetic person*, as our role picture of the personally effective individual. In analyzing the most common problems we human beings have in living effectively and productively, we will define this aiming point as specifically and as objectively as we can, in terms of what the meta-cybernetic person does. Then we can proceed to develop and practice the skills and techniques appropriate to that level.

breaking out of
the "amoeba" pattern

Probably everyone has, at one time, found himself in the amoeba pattern, drifting with circumstances, accepting one or more unsatisfactory situations in his life, and vaguely hoping for something better. Perhaps you've had some period in your life which you would look back on and describe as highly amoebic. Or, perhaps you would even characterize your present life situation as amoebic. Some people fall into this category in virtually all dimensions of their lives, and many more function amoebically in one or more specific dimensions such as career, home life, leisure activities, or self-development.

Breaking out of the amoeba pattern requires action — targeted, goal-oriented action to change specific circumstances for the better. This means forming the habit of thinking in terms of personal goals and doing specific things to reach them. Throughout much of the rest of this book, we will focus on this goal orientation and put it to direct use.

You can quickly get moving in a constructive direction again, in any or all areas of interest in your life, by making an "I want" list. Over a period of a few days to a few weeks, take a pen and paper and compile the longest possible list of things or conditions you would like to acquire. Include even the most far-out, impossible-sounding items, if you really feel you would enjoy having them. You needn't try to achieve all of the items on the list, but it will help you to make an inventory of the kinds of conditions you consider important for the quality of your particular life. Would you like a better job? A promotion? To go to work for yourself? A trip around the world? To learn to fly a plane? Run the marathon? Trace your family tree? Finish your formal education? Get elected to a political office? Get married? Get divorced? Renew your entire wardrobe? Learn photography? Act in a play? Make love with two people at once? Write a book or a magazine article? Take off thirty pounds? Buy a house?

Try to make your I-want list at least 100 items long, to make sure you consider various key result areas in your life. Include aspects of your present job, your career, your family life, your social activites, your physical health and conditioning, your cultural and creative activities, your hobbies, and any other category you consider important. Include also the items you might only go after at some far distant time in the future.

With an extensive I-want list, setting goals and making plans to reach them comes much more easily. Form the habit of organizing your personal activities and your work activities in terms of goals to the greatest extent possible. Describe what you plan to do in terms of a goal condition you will reach by completing the action. When you finish it, consciously acknowledge to yourself that you've achieved another goal. Check it off on your mental list, and take credit again for goal-oriented action.

Extend your thinking processes further into the future than you might typically do. What would you like to accomplish by six months from now? A year from now? Make some concrete plans with easily reachable steps, and get started carrying them out.

Moving from the amoebic level to at least the cybernetic level, as described previously, requires a commitment to setting goals, making plans, and taking action. This very soon becomes a successful habit, and one that brings its own rewards. The goal-oriented cybernetic pattern quickly becomes a self-reinforcing one. From there, the step to the meta-cybernetic level becomes much easier.

3

A PORTRAIT OF THE PERSONALLY EFFECTIVE INDIVIDUAL

what an effective individual does

The effective individual lives consciously. He achieves worthwhile results in his life by conscious thought and conscious action. While the amoebic individual reacts to the events and forces around him, the effective individual takes the initiative and makes things happen.

We can sum up the all-important difference between these two styles in terms of a fairly specific attitude — the *executive attitude*. While the amoebic individual considers the prime forces in his life as originating outside himself, the effective individual considers himself the prime force. He sees himself as the chief executive in his own life, with a concept of his life as an enterprise much like a corporation.

To act as the chief executive in one's own life means coming to terms confidently, assertively, and maturely with three basic factors:

1. *Authority* — the right to live and act in ways of one's own choosing. You have the authority to decide what to do with your life, how to organize it, whom to include in it, and how to manage it.

2. *Responsibility* — conscious acceptance of accountability to one's self for the consequences of one's action and for the present quality of one's life.

3. *Choice* — the basic process of moving through life, making choices among known or created alternatives for action. Choosing consciously what to do in dealing with any specific situation.

We shall explore the ramifications of each of these factors in greater depth as we proceed through the book. For the time being, let's recognize that they interact extensively and that acceptance of one of them implies acceptance of the other two. For example, to assume authority in one's life means to have the right to make the choices about living it. These choices bring with them certain consequences which you must also accept as a natural part of your responsibility for your life. We can describe this relationship as a triad of personal effectiveness factors, as in Figure 3–1.

Using this model, we can state an action-oriented, behavioral definition of personal effectiveness, as *a mode of action in which you maximize the quality of your life by assuming authority, accepting responsibility, and making choices, which you put into action to achieve those things and conditions that you personally value.*

In action terms, to function effectively means

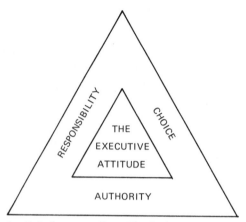

fig. 3-1: the executive attitude forms the foundation of personal effectiveness

that you specify what you want, decide what to do to get it, make plans, take actions, and overcome the obstacles that may stand in the way. These steps — specify, decide, plan, act — form a cyclic model as well, as illustrated in Figure 3-2. These two models taken together define the attitudes and actions of the effective individual.

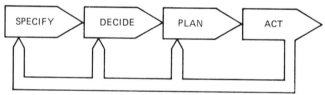

fig. 3-2: the effective person takes action and gets results

four basic competencies of personal effectiveness

For all of its apparent diversity, human ineffectiveness has certain basic defining patterns which we can observe by watching ineffective people operate. Their ineffectiveness really repeats only a few basic themes. And the highly effective person's behavior expresses mastery of the equivalent forms of competence in these basic areas. Anytime we slip away from our most effective modes of living, we tend to drift toward one or more of these basic forms of difficulty.

Actually, I believe we can divide virtually all of our "normal" malfunctions — those characteristic of basically "well-adjusted" people — into just four fundamental and interrelated categories, as follows:

14

1. *Adequacy* — problems with feeling capable, competent, effective, and potent. A person may conceive of himself as incapable or limited in some significant way, or perhaps even inadequate overall to meet the challenges of life. This self-limiting evaluation will show up in a relatively consistent way in the person's behavior.

2. *Approval* — problems with "what people think of me." A person with approval problems usually disapproves of himself strongly in one or more aspects and generally assumes that other people disapprove of him, look down on him, or consider him silly, incompetent, or otherwise unworthy. His behavior actualizes this self-assessment.

3. *Emotion* — problems in keeping one's emotional responses within reasonable bounds. The person with emotion problems may overreact to events and situations, or, alternatively, he may work so hard to suppress all evidence of his emotional functioning that he becomes emotionally flat and socially uninteresting. People we generally refer to as "moody" also have difficulty with the emotional dimension of their functioning.

4. *Values* — problems with doing what one really wants to do, as opposed to obeying the dictates of peers, family, husband, or wife, or the vaguely defined, invisible tyrants labeled "they" and "people." People who have allowed themselves to become trapped into unrewarding relationships or circumstances have value problems, and they often feel a vague sense of anger and resentment about their situations.

Those four categories of effectiveness and ineffectiveness suggest some corresponding categories of human competence, which we can define as the basic skills of personal effectiveness. I propose the following four areas of competence as defining categories which we can use to subdivide the subject into logical parts, which we can study, analyze, and learn:

1. *Mood control* — the psychomotor skill of maintaining a positive frame of mind and a correspondingly positive emotional bias in the vast majority of situations one encounters.

2. *Self-actualization* — actualizing one's own values; organizing one's life in such a way as to get what one really wants, rather than what one thinks others will approve of. This includes the process of learning, developing, and "improving" in one or more aspects of living which one cherishes.

3. *Social competence* — the various skills which enable one to get what one wants in dealing with other people and to maintain positive and rewarding interactions with them over the long term.

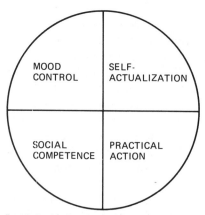

fig. 3-3: the basic competence model of personal effectiveness

      4. *Practical action* — the useful, everyday skills of getting results. This includes problem solving, making decisions, making plans, getting one's self and one's personal affairs well organized, and taking action to get things done.

      For the sake of memorizing these four areas of competence and for recalling them repeatedly as we progress through the following chapters, let's visualize them as in Figure 3-3. We will deal much more extensively with each of them and make an inventory of specific skills and techniques we can associate with each. All of these skills and techniques, taken together, constitute the mode of action we have defined as personal effectiveness.

taking stock of yourself

      Using the four-dimensional competence model of mood control, self-actualization, social competence, and practical action in Figure 3-3, you might want to make a constructive self-assessment at this point. On a scale of one to five, for example, how would you rate your personal effectiveness in each of the four areas?

      You might also find it useful to make a "forced-choice" ranking of the four areas. Without granting any tie scores, arrange the four competence areas in descending order of your own development. Which would you place first, and which fourth? On what basis did you make the ranking? What specific factors can you identify that constitute special strength areas? What specific aspects of any of the competence categories do you think warrant special attention or development?

16

After thinking it over as specifically as possible, review the four tables in Figures 3-4 to 3-7 and note some of the specific features of effectiveness and ineffectiveness in each of the four areas. If you've made your self-assessment a constructive one, you've probably acknowledged a number of special competencies you have. If not, maybe you need to think about the tendency to criticize yourself unduly and to set unrealistic self-evaluation criteria for yourself.

I strongly recommend that you avoid the cliche of "strengths and weaknesses." Focus on strengths at first and get a constructive, affirmative view of your competence. Then, if you like, identify specific areas in need of development. Refer to them as developmental areas rather than as weaknesses. This suggests action and improvement rather than condemnation.

From this general self-assessment, you can identify key areas of interest to you and set some priorities for aspects of your life you want to change. These changes might include developing certain skills more fully, solving certain problems, adding or eliminating things — or people — in your life, or a combination of all of these.

fig. 3-4: mood control

THE INEFFECTIVE PERSON	THE EFFECTIVE PERSON
Human ping-poing ball; has extreme and sudden ups and downs.	Keeps emotions on an even keel.
Loses temper easily.	Takes events and actions of others in stride.
Reacts irritably; snaps at others.	Reacts pleasantly and affirmatively.
Gets "wounded" or offended easily.	Declines to get "hooked" by provocative remarks or actions by others.
Does battle over small offenses.	Refuses to get drawn into useless and unproductive skirmishes with others.
Grim facial expression; negative emotional bias.	Maintains a positive emotional bias; smiles, expresses himself freely.
Little sense of humor.	Laughs easily; can laugh at himself.
Thinks predominantly negative, discouraged, or defeatist thoughts.	Keeps his mind on positive ideas, thinks about success, happiness, positive experiences.

fig. 3-4: mood control *(cont'd.)*

Suppresses all evidence of emotional responses.	Freely and exuberantly expresses himself.
Cries easily.	Laughs easily; cries seldom and for good reason.
Pouts, sulks.	Transacts as an adult.
Pays undue attention to bad news and negative subjects; talks or thinks himself into morbid moods.	Practices "input selection"; filters out or rejects morbid subjects unless he finds it necessary to deal with them.
Gets discouraged by small setbacks; lets small obstacles frustrate him.	Follows a flexible plan; accepts and adapts to setbacks; takes obstacles in stride, and adapts to surprises.
Often feels insignificant; dwells on failure rather than success.	Affirms himself; maintains a high level of self-esteem.

fig. 3-5: self-actualization

THE INEFFECTIVE PERSON	THE EFFECTIVE PERSON
Accepts peer values without question.	Examines peer values and evaluates their effectiveness for him.
Allows others to manipulate him with propaganda, advertising, etc.	Keeps his "crap detector" tuned in and working.
Censors his own thoughts and behavior, which others might consider unorthodox or "weird."	Freely questions the status quo, prevailing cultural values, and traditions; gives precedence to his own evaluations and choices.
Acts out socially expected "programs" of behavior, e.g., groupism, broadcasting status, sexual behavior, etc.	Outgrows programmed rituals; substitutues rewarding actions of his own choosing.
Sticks to known and familiar experiences.	Seeks and enjoys new experiences.
Avoids creative activities or those requiring unfamiliar skills	Tries new activities, undertakes activities that will teach him new skills.

fig. 3-5: self-actualization *(cont'd.)*

Neglects his education; seldom reads books, especially non-fiction; has little in the way of an intellectual life.	Reads, learns, acquires new ideas; thinks about abstract subjects and issues; diversifies his knowledge; takes courses, attends interesting lectures and seminars.
Seldom thinks about values, quality of life, purposes, or goals.	Frequently reviews his life and career; reaffirms his values, purposes, and goals; makes appropriate changes.

fig. 3-6: social competence

THE INEFFECTIVE PERSON	THE EFFECTIVE PERSON
Acts abrasively toward others.	Deals with others pleasantly, affirmatively, and constructively.
Manipulates others to get what he wants from them.	Declares his needs, wants, and preferences straightforwardly; negotiates for what he wants.
Allows others to manipulate him.	Decides clearly what he wants; eliminates guilt reactions, jealousy, etc.
Allows others to intimidate him.	Asserts his own rights, interests, and values; stands by his objectives and views.
Plays "games" with others; tries to induce guilt, jealousy, or dependency in others.	Negotiates openly to get what he wants; maintains a positive mood and doesn't need to get "one-up" on others.
Maintains a cold, distant exterior; withholds affirmation, affection, compliments, and greetings from others.	Maintains a positive, friendly manner; greets others, affirms them, shows affection appropriately.
Fawns on others; seeks praise or approval.	Approaches others as equals; gives and gets acceptance.
Puts others down, brags, scores "status points"; "one-ups" others.	Approaches others as equals; gives and gets acceptance.

fig. 3-6: social competence *(cont'd.)*

Forms overly dependent attachments, especially in relationships with the opposite sex; gets jealous, heart-broken, feels rejected when other person wants to discontinue.	Maintains a high sense of self-esteem; seeks other person's good will but does not depend on approval; can accept discontinuation without loss of self-esteem.

fig. 3-7: practical action

THE INEFFECTIVE PERSON	THE EFFECTIVE PERSON
Drifts; responds amoebically to events and actions of others. Allows his activities to become routine, patterned, and boring.	Has definite goals and plans for achieving them.
Avoids facing and dealing with problems and key issues.	Frequently reviews his activities and priorities; rearranges and renews them as necessary; finds new ways and new approaches. Confronts issues and identifies developing problems; solves problems, makes decisions, and takes action.
Allows others to impose unreasonable demands on his time, energy, and resources.	Manages his time effectively; focuses energy and resources on high-payoff areas of activity.
Procrastinates.	Gets things done according to priorities; uses time to advantage, meets deadlines with high-quality results.
Does little to organize his personal surroundings; has trouble finding things; squanders time on trivial and unproductive acitivities.	Maintains a personal "system"; has a personal "database"; manages time effectively; gets things done efficiently.
Feels frustrated by lack of "success" or "progress"; lacks specific criteria against which to evaluate his accomplishments.	Has specifically defined, realistic goals and priorities; compares progress against plans and takes satisfaction in his achievements.

GETTING ALONG
WITH YOURSELF

THERE AIN'T NO OZ

happiness myths

Most chronically unhappy people suffer more from their own misconceptions about happiness than from any specific circumstances or problems facing them in their lives. They tend to look upon their unhappiness as a state of their lives rather than a state of their minds. Such a person might very likely say, "I wish I could find happiness. I just want to be happy, but I can't seem to find it."

I call this the "Oz myth." Such a person seems to see himself as searching diligently for some happiness condition, some far-off place. He longs to travel to some personal never-never-land, an Oz where the Wizard will solve all his problems and give him the happiness he wants so desperately. He can't quite grasp the fact that Oz doesn't exist, it never did, and it never will. Just as in Frank Baum's famous story, *The Wizard of Oz*, where the various protagonists had to find their own solutions within themselves, the effective individual creates his own happiness by what he does.

The Oz myth can keep a person in a chronically unhappy and ineffective mode for a very long time. Only when he abandons this misconception and really grasps the fact that *happiness results from effective action* can he begin to reorganize his approach to the business of living. While suffering under the Oz myth, a person will tend to seek one situation or experience after another, hoping forlornly that *this* one will do it. This person, this love affair, this job, this town, this life-style, this group of friends will provide the happiness he feels entitled to. The unhappy person might reflect nostalgically on a previous period in his life, when he felt happier. "If only I could go back to that," he says to himself "I could be happy again." He may have enjoyed his job more, enjoyed his relationships more, or felt a higher sense of self-esteem in a dependent relationship with someone of the opposite sex.

Many chronically unhappy people also suffer from a similar myth, which psychologist Eric Berne labeled the "Santa Claus fantasy." According to Berne, such a person figuratively sits and waits, not enjoying life but doing little to change his circumstances, as if waiting for Santa Claus, or the good fairy, or Prince Charming, or some other unspecified magical person, who will come along and confer happiness on him. Both of these happiness myths come from the same erroneous assumption about happiness — that it comes from somewhere else or some outside agency, rather than from one's own actions. Berne, who specialized in colorful terms for describing human maladjustment, also liked to refer to this syndrome as "waiting in Destiny's bus station" for a bus that will supposedly come to take one to Oz.

These descriptions of happiness myths and the behavior patterns that go with them might seem overemphasized, but a large number of people do, indeed, suffer from the mistaken conceptions about happiness that underlie them. Of course, very few people would actually say, "I've chosen to wait here in Destiny's bus station, hoping that Santa Claus or somebody will come and make me happy." Yet, if you study the behavior patterns of chronically unhappy people, you can identify almost exactly this implied message in what they say and do.

Many of the social messages and cultural norms that surround us actually broadcast and reinforce these happiness myths. Many popular songs, for example, convey the notion that one becomes happy by falling in love with the right person. Titles like "You're Nobody 'Til Somebody Loves You," "My Life is Empty Without You," "I Can't Believe That You're In Love With Me," and "I Can't Live if Living Is Without You," all convey the message of dependency and the necessity of having some other person's approval and affection in order to feel significant. In the case of musical happiness myths, the loved one plays the part of Santa Claus, the good fairy, or Prince Charming.

The chronically unhappy person also tends to find convincing reasons for feeling unhappy. He will cite an unrewarding job, discouraging financial conditions, a lousy love affair, a problematical relationship with his family or friends, an inconsiderate boss, ill health, or personal shortcomings as evidence to support his conclusion that unhappiness has "happened" to him. Because he looks for reasons to feel unhappy, he finds them, and consequently he reaffirms his unhappiness.

The chronically happy person, on the other hand, starts with a different supposition. Because he has adopted the executive attitude about his life, he considers his own actions the primary source of his happiness. He has also learned that he can simply evaluate his personal circumstances in a positive way, paying attention to the encouraging aspects. He feels happy by choice, and he reinforces this feeling by finding more and more things to feel happy about. The chronically unhappy and the chronically happy persons proceed from two very different mental sets, each in a different direction.

The happy and effective individual realizes that Oz doesn't exist, and he understands that his own personal yellow brick road lies right under this feet, and it will take him anywhere he chooses to go.

Abraham Lincoln made a lot of sense when he remarked that "Most people are about as happy as they make up their minds to be."

the insane, the sane, and the unsane

Defining personal effectiveness as a mode of action makes it clear that the key to high-value results in any dimension of one's life lies in *adaptive* behavior. In any situation, one must find a course of action that leads to the results one wants. If you try some particular approach to a problem, such as a difficult job situation, and you don't like the results it brings, then you must try something else. The "value" of your behavior lies in its outcome. If you don't like the outcome, you'll have to change your behavior. The ability to adjust your behavior in response to a perceived outcome, and to keep doing this until you get some result which you value, constitutes a basic definition of psychological adjustment. Sanity, in its most basic, operational form, means the ability to adapt your behavior successfully to the situation at hand. In this respect, each of us behaves with some *relative degree of sanity*, rather than simply sanely or insanely.

Alfred Korzybski, the creator of the field of study known as general semantics, liked to describe human beings in three categories of relative sanity rather than as merely sane or insane. According to his view, we could categorize about fifteen percent of people as downright crazy. We lock them up or otherwise restrain them from circulating freely among the rest of us. At the other end of the scale, as illustrated in Figure 4-1, we have about fifteen percent of sane people, who have achieved a high level of adaptability. And in the middle of the bell curve, we have the merely "unsane" people — the normally maladjusted majority.

It makes much more sense to conceive of human adjustment—the foundation of personal effectiveness — as a distributed variable, such as the bell curve figure implies, rather than as an either-or proposition. People in the center of the scale constitute the great majority of people you meet. You yourself might fall into this category, in your own judgment or in the judgment of others who know you well. Much as I would like to flatter you, the reader, by assuming that you've developed a high level of sanity and personal effectiveness, the statistics of the situation suggest a seventy percent chance that you fall somewhere in the middle of the scale, at least in some aspects of your functioning.

fig. 4-1: a small number of people live and function at high levels of "sanity"

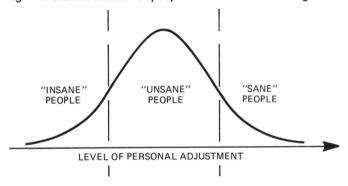

LEVEL OF PERSONAL ADJUSTMENT

Let's reflect for a moment on the implications of the term adaptive behavior. Most of us can adapt reasonably well to most of the obvious situations in life, like getting to work on time, or making a telephone call, or making a sale, or balancing a checkbook. The differences between the person of average effectiveness and the highly effective individual lie in the more subtle aspects of their interactions with the world and the people in it. They involve a level of functioning beyond the basics.

Having previously itemized some of the contrasting effective and ineffective behavior patterns associated with the four competence categories of mood control, self-actualization, social competence, and practical action, and recognizing that these patterns range along a continuum scale from highly ineffective to highly effective, we can now conceive of "personal growth" in a more specific, operational context. We can define personal growth as a matter of *acquiring skills*, specifically the various skills in each of the four key categories.

This view of personal growth, human adjustment, quality of life, and happiness as originating in skills and skill acquisition makes a great deal of practical sense, and it clearly points the way to action. We can apply the several models we've developed so far to the matter of acquiring these various competencies, and we can conceive of the process of increasing our personal effectivness as basically synonymous with "going sane."

THE DYNAMICS OF
SELF-ESTEEM

the basic concept
of self-esteem

The term *self-esteem* has become increasingly popular lately, and rightfully so. Most people sense, at least in a general way, that their attitudes toward themselves play a significant part in the ways in which they deal with the problems of living and in the levels of happiness they feel. Book titles like *How to Be Your Own Best Friend* and *The Psychology of Self-Esteem* testify to the increasing interest in self-esteem as an important aspect of one's approach to life.

In order to use the concept effectively, we need to give it a more explicit interpretation than it commonly enjoys in ordinary usage. Many people seem to use the term *self-esteem* with the connotation of a relatively abstract concept, in some way involving a feeling of "liking" one's self. We can use this notion effectively for our purposes, provided we support it with a behavioral point of view. We need to identify the specific behaviors associated with a low level of self-esteem and those associated with a high level of self-esteem. In this and later sections, I contend that a person can move from low esteem to high esteem just by *adopting the behavior of high esteem*. This makes it imperative to know what a person with high self-esteem does.

We can understand the general significance of the term *self-esteem* by first thinking about esteem, with respect to the attitudes we have toward other people. Each of us tends to have fairly definite personal reactions toward other people as individuals, and in their simplest form these reactions amount to attraction and rejection. To say you have a high esteem for another person implies that you feel a personal sense of attraction toward that person. If you hold someone in high esteem, you generally enjoy associating with him or her, or you would enjoy it if given the chance. You more or less "like" the person. Even if your high regard for the person centers on some specific professional or intellectual competence, you probably extend this high level of regard to the personal dimension of your relationship. We tend to like those people whom we admire.

Conversely, to say that you hold a person in low esteem, or that you have a relatively low regard for him or her, means that you feel a sense of repulsion or rejection toward that person. Regardless of particular reasons for your reaction, you generally feel disinclined to associate with that person. These general inclinations toward other people range along a broad scale, from repulsion through neutral, to attraction.

This overall assessment which you've made forms the basis for all of your continuing interactions with that person. You probably tend to approach your next interaction with the highly

28

esteemed person with the expectation of continuing to regard him or her highly, and you probably pay more attention to the positive aspects of the interaction than to those aspects that would invite you to change your assessment. Conversely, you probably deal with the minimally esteemed person with the expectation that your experiences will confirm your assessment, and you probably pay attention to the details of the interaction accordingly.

Now reverse this picture and think of *yourself* as the "other person" with whom you have to interact. You have adopted a very definite, although probably semiconscious, assessment of *yourself*. You tend to "like" yourself to some relative extent or other, based on some conclusions you drew about yourself a long, long time ago, and you tend to confirm those conclusions as you think about yourself and as you watch yourself in action. You might ask yourself, "If I didn't *have* to associate with me, to what extent would I consciously choose to do so?"

To get a clearer picture of your self-esteem, and to get around the elaborate rationalizations and self-descriptions you've given yourself over the years, you have only to study your own behavior objectively. By identifying your own high esteem behavior and low esteem behavior, you can infer reasonably well your own basic level of self-esteem. This understanding can then equip you to change your behavior if you choose to do so.

the concept
of personal power

If, at some time in your life, you faced an imminent disaster or even the possibility of sudden death, you can probably recall the feeling you had at that instant. You probably felt frightened, extremely anxious and aroused, and, above all, *powerless*. This feeling of helplessness, inadequacy, and impotence forms one extremity of the scale of a basic human emotion — the sense of significance, efficacy, and *personal power*. By personal power, I mean a fundamental, creature-level sense of potency, which plays an essential part in organizing your instantaneous responses to your environment.

At the other extreme of this wide scale, you can recognize the emotional high — the peak experience associated with winning, achieving, experiencing sudden good fortune, or achieving an exultant frame of mind leading to what some pychologists refer to as an "oceanic" feeling. At that moment, you feel extremely powerful. You feel a maximal sense of creature significance.

At other times, this emotional sensation of personal power fluctuates with your reactions to your circumstances. No matter what you do — getting out of bed, eating a meal, taking a walk, talking to someone, running from an angry dog, carrying out a complicated mental task, driving a car, listening to a boring lecture, making love, getting hired, getting fired, buying a pair of shoes — you have some instantaneous level of personal power. This feeling constitutes a basic "barometer" of your emotional state.

Note that this use of the term *power* does not include the connotations of social status, authority over others, or interpersonal influence. Personal power means your basic sense of creature efficacy, and it depends on your instantaneous *reaction* to your circumstances. Your internal power level might, of course, rise or decline in your dealings with other people, just as it fluctuates in various other situations.

Connecting this concept with some of our familiar experiences, we can establish some important links among self-esteem, personal power, and happiness level. When you sense a relatively high level of internal power in yourself, you probably would say, "I feel good." When your power level drops below some subjectively sensed level, perhaps because of extreme fatigue, hunger, or a negative emotional state, you might say, "I don't feel so good." With these comments, you report on the status of your power feeling.

Your power level responds to your thought processes. Think that statement over several times and see what possibilities it implies for consciously choosing to feel good. Most of us can, at certain times, voluntarily change our mood. You can probably boost yourself out of a discouraged mood on some occasions, simply by deciding to feel better. How do you do this? How, by a simple act of will, a neurological decision, did you increase your personal power level?

In terms of brain function and human neurological architecture, we still don't know. We do know that virtually anyone can do this, at least to some extent and in some circumstances. I contend that anyone can gain a significant measure of control of his or her emotional power level and keep it relatively high most of the time. Techniques for doing this constitute the category of personal effectiveness that I have labeled mood control.

You can think of your personal power level as reflecting two basic kinds of responses going on in your brain at all times, one automatic and the other perhaps "semiautomatic" and partially under your conscious influence. At the automatic level, your creature reaction to your perceptions of personal safety tends to dominate your power level. Faced with an attacking wild animal, an impending automobile crash, or an accidental fall from a high place, you would probably find it very difficult to remain calm, poised, and highly empowered. Your automatic survival reactions would probably dominate in such a situation.

Similarly perhaps, suddenly realizing you've

won a large sum of money might lead you to react strongly and automatically, moving to a high level of power feeling. Between these two extremes lie many, many experiences of the kind you have every single day. And you react to each of these experiences partly in an automatic way and partly by choice.

For example, as you live longer and learn more, you probably learn to take some provocations in stride. An experience that might have frustrated you in the past now might not arouse you at all, or you might have "demoted" it to the status of a mere nuisance. You did this by somehow changing the response pattern in your brain. Whatever neural pathway once triggered your anger and frustration, causing you to give away your personal power, now no longer has that effect. You have increased your mood control skill.

Think about the wide range of "automatic" negative reactions a person has. Fear, apprehension, anger, annoyance, embarrassment, worry — we use these words to describe varying aspects of the same sensation, the loss of a sense of personal power. Obviously, some people experience these feelings more often and more intensely than others, perhaps regardless of the relative number of difficult experiences they have. What constitutes a mere annoyance for one person may become a first-magnitude disturbance for another. When a person operates in this highly reactive, powerless mode much of the time, we recognize that he or she lacks an essential skill of adjustment. The person who maintains his or her feelings on an even keel most of the time has acquired not only the skill of taking things in stride, but also the psychomotor skill of maintaining a high internal power level.

We can combine these two very basic concepts, the concept of self-esteem and the idea of personal power, to form a practical approach to the skills of feeling happy. You can feel happy most of the time by consciously choosing to feel powerful and by adopting an attitude of high esteem toward yourself. These two basic approaches, along with the practical aspects of organizing and managing your life, enable you to function effectively in whatever you choose to do.

your self-estimate

Whatever level of self-esteem you have at this point in your life arises directly from your evaluation of yourself as a person — your comparison of yourself against some personal standard which you carry around in your mind. You probably arrived at this comprehensive self-estimate a long time ago and quite unconsciously, without recognizing the process by which you put it together. And you probably call upon it and reinforce it day-to-day, moment-to-moment, just as automatically. It forms the basis for virtually all that you do, all of your patterns and strategies for dealing with other people, your views of your capabilities, and your personal "theory" about how to get whatever you happen to want.

Your personal self-estimate forms just as much an integral part of "you" as your voice, your hair color, your height, and the shape of your nose. Whether you think consciously about your view of yourself, you do, indeed, call upon this patterned self-concept consistently and routinely all through your life.

Because the self-estimate has such a profound influence on one's behavior and consequently on one's personal effectiveness, we would do well to understand how it gets formed and how one can change it. We can understand the self-estimate clearly in terms of the following facts about it:

1. A person starts forming his self-estimate very early in childhood, perhaps as soon as he becomes aware of himself as a separate, differentiated human being.

2. This process goes on for a number of years, and it goes on continuously and quite unconsciously, largely at the intuitive, preverbal level.

3. The vast majority of adults retain throughout their entire lives essentially the same self-estimates they had adopted by late adolescence or their early teens.

4. Some people develop extremely negative or defeating self-estimates as a result of disaffirming experiences in early childhood or adolescence.

5. A much smaller number of people develop highly positive self-estimates as a result of affirmative, supportive experiences in childhood, with parents and other adults who knew how to raise them in a positive way.

6. A small number of people become sufficiently conscious of their self-estimates and the associated behavior patterns that they deliberately revise and improve them.

7. A person's self-estimate forms the basis for his choice of strategies for getting what he wants, and particularly for getting feelings of personal power as we have defined it above.

Let's trace, in very brief form, the childhood time-line, and see how your own early experiences probably predisposed you toward one kind of self-estimate or another.

In the first few months of life, you had no intellectual faculties to speak of, and consequently you took in "raw" sensory data. Sights, sounds, tastes, smells, tactile sensations, and body contact with your mother and/or other significant adults formed the primary substance of your perceptions. From this physical contact especially, you derived an intuitive, preverbal impression of love and physical affection. You got a certain supply of it, ranging from very little to very much, and you recorded neurologically your reactions to it.

As you moved into early babyhood, from about six months to about two years, you began to form rudimentary preverbal concepts and intuitive conclusions about the people and things you could see. You learned a primitive repertoire of behaviors that seemed to work for you in getting your basic needs met — needs for food, physical comfort, and affection. You learned two contrasting repertoires of feelings, those referred to by Eric Berne as "OK" feelings and "not-OK" feelings. You had those feelings as automatic reactions of need-satisfaction and need-deprivation. You sensed the relative level of love available from the giants who populated your life, and you tried to get it in whatever ways seemed to work.

By about age two, when you began to acquire your language skills at a rapid rate, you had also become mobile and at least marginally competent in basic motor skills. You began exploring your world extensively, and you began putting together some sort of a cause-and-effect theory about how the world works. By this time, you had firmly embedded in the shadowy regions of your preverbal experience the intuitive concepts of powerfulness and powerlessness, affection and hostility on the part of yourself and others, acceptance and rejection of yourself by others, and a general "comfort zone" of experience within which you felt reasonably adequate, safe, and happy. On top of this primitive conceptual structure, you began rapidly to overlay certain verbal concepts you started to acquire. Words like good and bad began to take on a rudimentary meaning to you, along with your perceptions of the nonverbal signals the adults transmitted when they used those terms.

Certain things the adults did frightened you, and you learned certain behavioral responses, like crying, to get them to stop. Other things they did made you feel very good, and you learned to give them whatever signals seemed necessary to get them to continue. Many things in your world utterly baffled you. Many things treacherously attacked you, injured you, frightened you, and frustrated you. Many of the signals coming from the adults consisted of "don't messages." "Don't do that, dear." "Don't pull kitty's tail." "Don't put the fork in the light socket." "Don't touch the television." You realized beyond a shadow of a doubt that the giants made all the rules in the world, and they had infinite power to enforce them. Your primary task during this period became that of finding a set of strategies for getting what you wanted out of the adults and for dissuading them from annihilating you.

At this critical stage in your life, you began to sense, again largely in preverbal intuitive form, what the big people in your particular world thought of you and how they felt toward you. You probably heard them use a wide variety of words in talking to you, and some of those words you heard repeatedly. You realized in a vague way that those words described you, much as your name described you. If you had highly critical, hostile, or immature parents, you might have heard such words as stupid, dummy, clumsy, brat, bad, nasty, and so forth. If you had highly mature, loving, and caring parents, you might have heard such words as I love you, you're good, you're special, that's good, and the like. You began to develop a descriptive picture of yourself, based largely on the words used by the giants and connected to your preverbal impressions of affection, rejection, fear, pleasure, and adequacy. You developed, in the words of psychologist Harry Stack Sullivan, a *reflected self-estimate* — a picture of yourself as seen in the mirror of the actions and responses of the big people toward you.

You put together this primitive preliminary definition of yourself, a hodgepodge of verbal and preverbal concepts, much of it conflicting and confusing, based largely on the accident of fate which placed this particular group of giants in your young life at that time. You can easily see from this description the massive impact that the parent's level of maturity has on the child's eventual self-estimate, and consequently his self-esteem. One or more poorly adjusted, ineffective parents in a young child's life will usually send him more negative signals than positive ones. He will probably have a larger diet of angry, hostile treatments by the big people than positive, loving treatments. They may reject him, ignore him, physically abuse him, ridicule him, or intimidate him in their clumsy struggles to meet their own emotional needs by means of the crude and ineffective strategies they have learned.

Conversely, one or more well-adjusted, highly effective people as parents will probably give him plenty of love and physical affection, nurture him, teach him, reward his successes and not criticize failures, support him when he needs support, affirm him as a worthwhile human being, and grant him the freedom to grow up at his own comfortable speed.

Returning to the time-line, we see you emerging from early childhood into early adolescence at about age five. By this time, you had fairly well come to terms with the big people in your life. You had studied their behavior very actively, and you had worked out a fairly reliable theory of their actions and motivations. You had learned to get along with them reasonably well. As you eagerly and spontaneously pursued your learning process, you began to acquire more sophisticated and somewhat more abstract concepts, including a concept of yourself as their little boy or girl, of whom they had certain expectations. By now, they had conveyed to you a fairly detailed picture, although probably not consciously or methodically, of what they wanted you to become. They gave you a wide variety of evaluative signals, which told you the extent to which you matched up with their expectations for you. Because you needed their attention, love, and affection, to say nothing of their food and the security of their protection, you became what you needed to become at this point in your life.

As you left your home for your first public school experiences, you came in touch with many other little people like you, all going through the same process of working out a theory of life, and you also came face to face with the first of many additional authority figures who would populate your life — teachers and other significant adults. At this point, the central dynamic in your life became the processes of *evaluation* and *conformity*. By this time, the big people considered you sufficiently grown up to begin learning how to function as a little citizen in the environment they had created for you. They showed you how they expected you to behave, they punished you when you defied those norms, and they rewarded you when you abided by them. They provided a socialization process for you, by which you learned how to function reasonably well in civilized society.

To a great extent, your self-estimate at this point centered on this little citizen role, together with the accumulated conceptual structure you brought with you out of your early childhood stage. You may have drawn certain distinct conclusions about yourself, based almost entirely on the inputs you received from the big people in their dealing with you. These might range all the way from highly affirmative inputs, such as statements about your special skills or attributes, to the highly negative or critical, such as derogatory terms and discouraging or condemnatory statements about your capabilities or potentials. All of these inputs became part of the emotional luggage which you would probably carry with you for the rest of your life.

At this point, the time-line of possibilities for the development of your self-estimate becomes too diversified and multifarious for us to trace the variations. You probably began to deal with other children, to test and evaluate your motor skills, athletic skills, social skills, artistic and musical skills, and intellectual skills, and to compare yourself with other children. You formed some distinct opinions about your "strengths" and "weaknesses," particularly your weaknesses. You began to favor those skills and activities you could do well and to avoid those in which you failed or experienced embarrassment or humiliation.

Out of the infinite variety of opinions you could possibly have adopted about yourself, you progressively reduced the field to a few basic ones. These became the core of your self-estimate — your *evaluative definition* of yourself as a person. The sum total of your adolescent experiences led you to a fairly definite view of yourself, your capabilities, and your worth as a human being. From there on, life became largely a matter of adding years and gaining competence in that relatively narrow range of processes you had chosen for your life. If your life has followed the same general trend of probably eighty-five percent of people, you still have today roughly the same self-estimate you had constructed by the time you had moved well into your teenage years. Your strategies for meeting your needs then have probably become, for the most part, your strategies for meeting your needs now.

the great irony
of self-esteem

Psychologist Eric Berne, who developed the system of transactional analysis, believed that all human beings arrive at about age five or six with roughly similar self-estimates, varying only in the details of their formulation. He believed that every child, virtually without exception, experiences his early life as a struggle with a vast array of confusing and overpowering forces beyond his control. Even with the most mature, loving, and personally effective parents, the little person cannot transcend his own ineptness. The primitive level of his neurological development, as well as his small size, condemn the little person to feelings of incompetence and powerlessness much of the time. Berne referred to this inescapable situation as the "childhood dilemma."

As a result of this, according to Berne, the child arrives at age five or six with a distinct sense of his own limitedness, especially when he compares himself with the omnipotent giants of whom

the "childhood dilemma": small, inept, and dependent

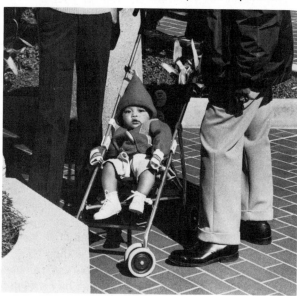

he lives in awe. Berne summed up this initial *life position* as a conclusion that everybody else in the world — namely the adults — has infinite power and efficacy, and that he alone has virtually none. In the vernacular of transactional analysis, this translates to a life position summarized as "I'm not-OK, but you're OK." The term *OK*, used in this sense, implies a broad and uncritical judgement about significance and efficacy — in short, about personal power. The five-year-old concludes that he somehow got short-changed when they handed out the power, that everybody else in the world got a big share while he got none.

Furthermore, Berne theorized, the little person begins to build his entire repertoire of transactional strategies on this assumptive foundation. As he grows older, he may or may not revise this self-estimate, based on the kinds of experiences he has and his acquired ability to learn from those experiences and to synthesize more effective strategies. Unfortunately, according to Berne, all but a small fraction of people continue to cling to this basic assumption about themselves in comparison with others. They grow into their adult years with the unrecognized and unverbalized notion that everybody else in the world counts for more than they do. Indeed, Berne claimed, probably ninety percent of human beings go to their graves with the same "one-down" view of themselves that they had at age five or six. Fewer than ten percent make the conscious intellectual and emotional leap which transcends the childhood life position and lays claim to the power and privileges of the "OK" life position.

If you consider this developmental phenomenon with respect to a large number of people, you will probably sense the profound irony of a bunch of not-OK people trying to deal with one another. As Figure 5–1 illustrates, person A assumes "I'm not-OK, but you're OK." His behavior will manifest this view of general "one-downness" in his dealings with the other person. Person B holds exactly the same assumption — "I'm not-OK, but you're OK." This reciprocal one-down position will lead him to behave in particular ways toward person A, probably with his own creative variations. Here we have two one-down people transacting some kind of business, with each unconsciously granting the other a higher degree of personal worth and assumed potency than he grants to himself.

I call this phenomenon the great Irony of Self-Esteem, and we can see it at work every day in the transactions people have with one another.

Perhaps this discussion has led you to reflect on your own general level of self-esteem and to identify more explicitly some of the key features of your own self-estimate. If so, you might want to shift certain aspects of your self-estimate in a more positive direction and increase your overall level of personal power and self-esteem. Several of the following chapters offer specific techniques for doing that.

fig. 5-1: the great irony of self-esteem

the two basic varieties of low self-esteem

A person with a negative self-estimate, and consequently a low level of self-esteem, nevertheless needs to accomplish his ends and get along in the world. He adopts, therefore, some repertoire of behaviors that he believes will help him get what he wants, subject to the limitations he has imposed on himself. The low-esteem person tries, most of all, to avoid those situations or experiences which he thinks will emphasize his sense of ineptness and cause him to feel powerless or underpowered. He protects his ego by any of a wide variety of behavioral strategies, while trying to achieve whatever ends he has in mind.

As the low-esteem person assembles the basic repertoire of behavioral strategies which he will probably use for the rest of his life, he tends to move in one of two primary directions, but not both. On one hand, he may choose, usually unconsiously, a set of behaviors we will call the behaviors of *capitulation*. He figuratively "gives in" to those around him and accepts whatever the world deems fit to offer him. The shy, self-effacing person provides the best example of this behavioral style. Those who have significant doubts about their ability to function effectively among other people often choose the capitulative style. They don't make waves, they don't challenge or confront other people, and they don't take risks. The philosophy behind the capitulative style says, "Cut your losses, play the game with minimal stakes, and hope for the best."

Conversely, some people adopt a contrasting pattern of behavior, characterized by highly demonstrative, aggressive, or acquisitive actions. The pattern of *compensation* has the aim of deceiving other people, and principally one's self, about what one considers his most damning weaknesses and inadequacies. These people project a phoney form of bravado and apparent self-confidence. They often talk loudly, forcefully, or aggressively, and they pressure other people with various tactics which help them acquire feelings of personal power by getting one-up on others.

We can array these two contrasting low-esteem behavioral styles, capitulation and compensation, at the extremes of a continuum scale, as in Figure 5–2. The capitulator seems to say with his behavior, "Yes, world. You're right. I am indeed worthless and insignificant. I expect you to treat me that way. I won't ask for anything more than you choose to give me." Conversely, the compensator seems to say with his behavior, "You're wrong, world. I am not worthless and insignificant, and I'll prove it to you. I'll make you notice me, accept me, and respect me." The capitulator behaves passively, the compensator aggressively.

Ironically, both the capitulator and the compensator proceed from the same negative suppositions about their worthlessness and insignificance, even though they adopt radically different strategies. The capitulator tries to opt out of the game, choosing to sit along the sidelines and watch everyone else play, while the compensator charges onto the playing field aggressively and clumsily, trying to score points in any way he can.

Typical capitulating behaviors include:

fig. 5-2: the contrasting behavioral "styles" of capitulation and compensation both originate in low self-esteem

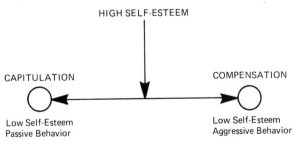

HIGH SELF-ESTEEM

CAPITULATION   COMPENSATION

Low Self-Esteem   Low Self-Esteem
Passive Behavior   Aggressive Behavior

1. Keeping silent, speaking rarely and cautiously.
2. Speaking tentatively, hesitantly, or apologetically.
3. Avoiding eye contact with others.
4. Avoiding highly social situations, avoiding having to meet new people.
5. Giving in routinely to the wishes or demands of others.
6. Changing one's mind at the slightest urging of someone else.
7. Avoiding or evading conflict, controversy, or confrontation with others.
8. Failing to take initiative to get what one wants from others.
9. Surrendering one's rights or objectives with aggressive or domineering people.
10. Sticking to safe, routine, and familiar experiences; avoiding adventures or unfamiliar and challenging experiences.

Typical compensating behaviors include:

1. Talking a great deal, talking loudly, and using dogmatic language.
2. Broadcasting artificial status by showing off expensive cars, clothes, jewelry, home, or other material possessions.
3. Dropping names, bragging, scoring "status points" or "success points" in conversation.
4. Trying to dominate or intimidate others with eye contact or other nonverbal behavior.
5. Putting others down, ridiculing them, or insulting them.
6. Displaying inappropriately aggressive social behavior, such as swearing, telling off-color jokes, or otherwise violating generally accepted norms of good taste.
7. Seeking group situations as forums for constant socializing and earning approval from others.
8. Making unfair or unreasonable demands of others.
9. Intruding on the privacy of others, imposing one's company without invitation.
10. Undertaking an endless variety of achievement-oriented activities, trying to earn the respect and admiration of others.

The compensator usually does a better job of hiding his faulty self-estimate, especially from himself, than the capitulator does. For this reason, many compensators pass reasonably well for high-esteem people, unless you look more closely. With the capitulator, however, you can easily see what kind of self-estimate he has adopted. Capitulators often look upon extreme compensators with awe, assuming that they have infinite confidence in themselves, and that they must possess very high levels of self-esteem. Because the capitulator feels he could never bring himself to behave in the aggressive, outgoing style of the compensator, he feels that the compensator has, somehow, "made it." He usually doesn't stop to look closely at the compensator's behavior and to realize that the compensator has become just as imprisoned by his faulty self-estimate as he, the capitulator, has.

Most people express their self-estimates rather clearly when it comes to the matter of sexuality. The capitulator generally tends toward careful control and de-emphasis of his or her sexuality, preferring to broadcast as little as possible in the way of sexual "signals." The compensator, on the other hand, may tend to overemphasize sexuality and sexually oriented behavior, much as he or she overemphasizes other aspects of personal significance.

The "macho" behavior pattern among males constitutes a special case of compensation. Young men especially, most of whom harbor substantial doubts about their masculinity, tend to display the characteristic swaggering pattern and stern facial expression which signals potential aggressiveness and territorialism. Psychologist Alfred Adler studied this phenomenon extensively and he concluded that it stems from a fundamental creature-level anxiety about subjugation and loss of potency. Adler termed this highly compensatory behavior pattern the "masculine protest," implying that the young male tries to deny behaviorally an assumed one-down status with respect to other males.

Incidentally, the characteristic bravado and aggressiveness of this "John Wayne syndrome" constitutes a set of signals aimed not at females, but *at other males*. The signals have the purpose of keeping other males more or less at a safe distance and of masking one's own feelings of anxiety and insecurity. Most postpubescent males have learned an extensive array of "potency" behaviors, ranging from locker room slang to sexually oriented jokes, to nonverbal signals and postures that convey dominance or territorial possession, all the way to physically aggressive or combative actions. Typically, a man who displays a pronounced macho orientation in the presence of other males will switch to a much softer, less aggressive, and more socially cautious pattern when he finds himself alone in the presence of several females.

In any town or airport near a military base, you can usually see young recruits, lonely and away from home, bravely "advertising" what they can't quite buy themselves — the idea that they have attained full manhood. Recruiting posters, especially those for the Marine Corps, pander blatantly to this deep-seated masculine anxiety.

Young police officers also tend toward the behaviors of masculine protest. The swaggering, confident-appearing

the "macho" behavior pattern expresses the "masculine protest" against feelings of insecurity and uncertainty about masculinity

"Wyatt Earp" syndrome of the new officer compensates for the very real sense of uncertainty and anxiety which comes with this new, strange, and unfamiliar role.

Virtually everyone, whatever his level of self-esteem, tends to retreat to one of the two styles, capitulation or compensation, in threatening situations. Although every person has tendencies to compensate as well as capitulate when he finds his feelings of personal power in jeopardy, the vast majority of people lean at least slightly toward one of these two distinct styles as a general orientation. People with highly negative self-estimates lean furthest toward the extremes. Indeed, you can infer the general level of positiveness of another person's self-estimate simply by assessing the extent to which he or she displays the characteristic behaviors of either of the two primary styles.

Which of these styles do *you* tend toward when you get into uncomfortable or socially threatening situations? Would you describe your behavior in normal situations as more or less centered on the continuum scale? Or, might you consider yourself to have developed one of these two orientations extensively, such that you might

42

want to make some changes in your self-estimate and in your corresponding behavioral style?

The behavioral point of view we're using in this book makes it difficult to delude yourself about your actual self-estimate. Pay little attention to what you say to yourself about your self-esimate; just pay attention to what you do. You can believe your behavior.

the shyness syndrome

We can see an extreme version of the capitulation style in the behavior of people we generally refer to as "shy." Have you noticed certain common features in the behaviors of shy people you know? Extremely shy people have so much in common, behaviorally speaking, that we can correctly identify shyness as a behavioral *syndrome* — a characteristic pattern of interrelated elements.

The characteristic behavioral strategy of the shy person centers around one word — "don't." The shy person almost tries not to exist. He avoids intruding or imposing on others, avoids getting into disagreements or conflicts with others, and seldom voluntarily initiates social contacts without a very compelling reason. Many shy people have a characteristic "vanilla" personality, a dull, flat style which doesn't offend, doesn't arouse, doesn't catch the attention. A shy person will usually speak in a quiet, controlled voice, generally with a pronounced monotone.

Such a person can sit for an hour or more in a business meeting, listening to other people shoot off their mouths about subjects they don't understand, and never once speak up to share what he knows. When spoken to, he will usually say as little as possible, as tentatively as possible, and will signal by tone of voice and inflection that he will not object if interrupted, overruled, or disagreed with. Shy people virtually apologize for existing. They do not expect others to take them seriously, and they act out this expectation.

Shy people usually avoid taking risks in most areas of their lives, not just in the social dimension. They generally fear failure almost as much as they fear rejection and disapproval by other people. They typically center their lives on a few trustworthy activities and processes from which they can derive a measure of satisfaction and feelings of significance, and steer clear of the rest. They often seek jobs or careers in fields that require minimal interaction with other people.

The shyness syndrome comes from a very distinctive pattern of childhood experience. The shy person, almost without exception, experienced a great deal of criticism and intimidation by the big people in his life during the period when he formed and "froze" his self-estimate. The giants of his early life, typically his natural parents and to a greater or lesser extent other significant grown-ups, handed out a steady diet of three especially toxic kinds of treatment: *scolding*, *criticism*, and *disaffirmation*. They told him, directly and indirectly, verbally and nonverbally, and on a continuing basis, that they considered him worthless, inept, and unlovable. They systematically undermined his sense of confidence and personal significance.

And, of course, he believed it. As we've seen, the young person forms a reflected self-estimate based on the predominance of signals transmitted to him by the big people in his early life. *Toxic treatment by grown-ups almost invariably produces a shy adolescent, who usually grows up to become a shy adult imprisoned by the same faulty self-estimate for the rest of his life.*

In personal effectiveness seminars, I've often heard shy people "defend" their parents against the implied criticism that this explanation entails. Yet, on careful reflection, they often realize with considerable consternation — and frequently some hostility — just how poorly and unlovingly their parents treated them as a general matter.

Even if the shy person's parents do somehow deserve blame for producing a shy adolescent, the shy person himself bears the responsibility for remaining shy. He has carried a primitive, negative, and limiting self-estimate from his adolescent period right on into his adult years. Perhaps as an adolescent he did seem to himself inept, incapable, and unlovable. But as an adult he should know better. Because he never bothered to review and revise his childhood self-estimate, he continues to ignore the contrary evidence and to search for — and find — the confirmatory evidence. He considers himself inferior, he acts it out, and he proves it to himself every day.

increasing your self-esteem

Possibly you've decided that your self-estimate and your general sense of self-esteem could use a bit of a boost. Probably every human being could profit by paying more attention to his self-esteem and deliberately acting to enhance it. Your need to increase your self-esteem might range from slight to great. You might want to virtually rebuild your self-estimate, or you might merely want to "fine tune" it.

In order to make some deliberate changes, it helps to identify your characteristic behavioral style in terms of capitulation or compensation. Which of the two primary orientations do you use most often, and how extensively do you display them?

In reflecting on your orientation, remember that the capitulator generally has a more accurate view of his own behavior than the compensator does, because the compensator has learned to fake himself out as well as others. So, if you hear yourself saying that your self-esteem needs no changing, not even any fine tuning, you might investigate the possibility that you have firmly acquired the compensator style.

A thoughtful behavioral self-inventory will give you a pretty good answer. Think about the ways you organize your life, the challenges you set for yourself, the extent to which you meet others halfway, and the extent to which you treat others positively and affirmatively. Your "crisis" behavior, that is, the way you typically respond to conflict or pressure situations, will also help you to understand your self-estimate. The two prime options of "fight" and "flight" describe, in general terms at least, the two primary patterns of compensation and capitulation. Sit back for a few moments and mentally "watch" yourself go through a typical working day, as well as typical social or interpersonal activities. How do you relate to coworkers? Other peers? Your boss? Your employees, if you manage? Other authority figures? Customers or clients? Mate or romantic partner? Children?

This inventory might identify two or three key behaviors you would like to abandon and two or three you would like to adopt. The more specifically and operationally you state these behaviors, the more effectively you can abandon or adopt them. Instead of using indefinite terms like "be more friendly," try using operational statements like "greet each person in the office in the morning," "say hello to strangers on the street," "look people in the eye when I talk to them," and "invite coworkers to join me for coffee more often." Instead of "be more considerate of others," try phrasing it as "allow others to finish their sentences when they talk to me," "stop making fun of others and putting them down with verbal barbs," "listen carefully and attentively when others speak," "solicit their ideas and viewpoints," and "give positive strokes to others." In every case, keep revising it until you feel you have identified a specific, observable, and changeable behavior on your part. Then it becomes a fairly simple matter to keep the new behavior pattern in mind as often as possible and shift toward it more and more every day.

We can subdivide the overall process of building self-esteem into four general strategies:

1. Consciously boosting your personal power feelings frequently and routinely throughout the day, using the techniques explained in Chapter 6.

2. The "act-as-if" policy — adopting target behaviors associated with the higher level of self-esteem you want to attain.

3. Restating your self-estimate in grown-up terms, eliminating self-defeating and self-condemning statements about yourself, adopting positive and self-affirming statements.

4. Acknowledging and taking credit for your strengths, accomplishments, and resources at every turn, as well as taking note of every improvement in your self-esteem.

Specific strategies for carrying out this esteem-building process will vary according to individual behavioral styles, and you must choose your own distinctive approach. Compensators need somewhat different change strategies than capitulators do, because they have to move in radically different directions.

The compensator needs to ease up, relax, learn to laugh at himself, take credit for his accomplishments, accept and approve of himself, stop crashing into situations at full power, perhaps talk less, listen more, learn, adapt to others, compromise when necessary, stop one-upping others, and adopt positive, supportive behaviors toward other people. He needs to develop a demeanor of quiet, subtle self-confidence and self-acceptance, and he will begin to actually feel that way more and more.

The capitulator needs to come out of his cave and deal with the world forthrightly and courageously, face and solve problems — especially human and interpersonal ones — act directly rather than deviously or manipulatively to get his needs met, assert his right to live and function with the same adult status as every other human being, take risks, say "no" when he wants to say it and say "yes" when he wants to say it, and to take the initiative in dealing with other people. By *acting* confidently and assertively, the capitulator soon *becomes* more confident and assertive and feels less and less need to avoid and evade.

The special case of the shy person warrants much more extensive study than space allows here, but a shy person can indeed improve his self-estimate and adopt more powerful behaviors. I usually advise the shy person to undertake a self-chosen *adventure* of some kind, in which he will find it necessary to cope with a challenging and demanding situation unlike any other he has faced in the past. He might join a Toastmasters Club and learn to stand up in front of others and express his ideas, take a trip to a foreign country alone without joining a tour group, get elected head of the PTA, fly a plane, run a marathon, or any of a vast number of other challenging experiences. It doesn't really matter what adventure he selects, so long as he finds it at least a little bit scary but generally feasible. The mere act of adventuring will teach him that he *can* do more than he thought he could and that he can probably succeed at other challenges. A major personal adventure has the effect of kicking the shy person out of his rut of self-confirming low-esteem and getting him moving toward a much stronger self-estimate.

A shy person can also increase his sense of personal power and self-esteem by the technique of *graduated behavior programming*. If you consider yourself a very shy person, put the following recipe to use for a few weeks or months and note the results.

First, make a list of a large number of fairly specific and moderately "risky" behaviors, emphasizing social situations; these might include giving an opinion at a staff meeting, calling up someone to invite them for a date, disagreeing with someone, sending back an inferior plate of food in a restaurant, saying "no" to an inconsiderate request for a favor, turning down an invitation without offering a reason or an excuse, accepting a compliment straightforwardly and without "cancelling" it with a counter-statement, or smiling at a stranger.

Next, rank-order these behaviors from lowest risk to highest risk according to your own personal experience and your own reactions. Which of them offers the greatest threat to your self-esteem? Which of them could you adopt with just a little effort, without going too far out on a limb? For example, if volunteering an opinion in a staff meeting terrifies you, try simply asking a question. This might give you a way to start talking — a basic assertive behavior — without having to worry about disagreement or disapproval from others. You might put this action near the top of your list of feasible new behaviors.

Once you have the list, use it on a daily basis as a plan for acting more and more assertively while staying within your comfort zone. Begin to actually do the things at the top of the list. As you go along, adopting more of the previously risky behaviors, you'll find your comfort zone getting larger and larger, so that you become less imprisoned in the shyness syndrome and more able to act — and become — confident. If you begin literally to impersonate a confident person, you will become that person.

MOOD CONTROL
SKILLS

managing your mood

Stand on a busy street corner sometime and watch the expressions on the faces of people going by. Watch their overall demeanor, their bearing, and the ways they walk. Do you sense a relative level of positive or negative mood in the face of each person? Why do some people seem to feel positive, potent, and basically cheerful, while others seem to project a sour, angry, downtrodden, or irritable mood?

Certainly, each person's mood will fluctuate to some extent according to his experiences, and some of the people you observe might feel momentarily happy or out of sorts. But we know that some people seem to feel out of sorts a great deal of time, while others seem to feel basically happy and positive a great deal of time. Those in the latter category have learned the specific skill of mood control, which as we discussed in Chapter 3, is the ability to maintain a relatively positive frame of mind and an associated positive emotional state most of the time.

Reflect for a moment on the meaning of the term *moody*. When we describe someone as moody, we usually mean that he or she spends a great deal of time in negative moods. We also usually mean that his or her mood can change rather suddenly, and often with relatively little apparent provocation. The "ping pong" person, who goes from elation to despair in reaction to ordinary daily events, qualifies for the label of moody. He has trouble with mood control. It seems as if the "cause" of his mood comes from outside sources rather than from his own mental processes. Most of us find moody people relatively unattractive as social partners, as well as working colleagues. How many people with mood control problems have you seen inappropriately assigned to public contact jobs, such as waitress, bank teller, retail clerk, or receptionist?

Choose a few moody people you know and watch them through a typical day's activities. How do they respond to the situations that arise? How do they deal with obstacles, setbacks to their progress, and uncooperative people? What general mood level do they maintain throughout the day? Similarly, study a few highly positive people through a day's activities and note their reaction processes and mood levels. How do they seem to keep themselves in a positive frame of mind?

Do you consider yourself a moody person? Do others? On an imaginary scale ranging from one to ten, with ten meaning a very positive mood, where would you place your long-term average mood level? Do you go about with a grim, firmly set expression on your face and a rigid body posture most of the time, or do you have a flexible expression, smile often, and move your body freely and gracefully? How would you rate your sense of humor? Do you appreciate a joke? Can you tell one well? Can you joke and laugh in a positive way with others? Can you laugh at yourself and with yourself, not putting yourself down and yet not taking yourself entirely seriously? Do you respond to others cheerfully and positively?

Think of your mood level as your subjectively sensed status of your brain and nervous system, which gives you a general indication of the relative positiveness of your frame of mind at any one moment. The skill of mood control amounts to the ability to monitor your mood, change your frame of mind as necessary to keep it generally positive, and boost your feelings of personal power to bring your mood level up, all without necessarily having a "reason," that is, an external happening in your world which "makes" you feel happy.

Does the idea of mood control seem vaguely indecent to you? Does the notion of deliberately exchanging a negative emotional set for a positive one seem somehow like cheating your feelings or manipulating yourself? To some people, the idea of changing their own feelings ranks on a par with infanticide, somehow "unnatural." Probably the current preoccupation with personal growth movements, especially the more narcissistic ones which urge personal transparency and emotional incontinence, have contributed to a fuzzy notion of feelings as fully automated responses to outside events, especially the doings of other people. This point of view portrays emotions of all kinds as good and desirable — the more the better. The most sophisticated one-up strategy these days has one person avowing that he can emote more than someone else can. Mood control may not make much sense to those who hold this view.

Most of us, however, probably accept the notion that we ourselves influence our own mood much of the time, largely by the particular frame of mind we adopt and by the ways in which we *choose* to respond to our experiences. Think of mood control as a *psychomotor skill* which you can practice and develop. Make it a habit to tune in to your overall mood many times each day. See how you've chosen to feel, decide whether you want to feel that way, and if not take conscious action to raise your mood level.

positive thoughts and positive feelings

Norman Vincent Peale once commented, "Change your thoughts and you change your world." By this he meant that you change your *perception* of the world, which for all practical purposes amounts to the same thing.

By maintaining a generally positive frame of mind most of the time, you can maintain and enjoy a positive mood most of the time. Let's explore some of the specific implications of the term "frame of mind" and identify some specific things you can do to keep it positive.

Let's define frame of mind as the overall *orientation* of your thoughts, including what you think about at any one moment and the extent to which the subject matter of your thinking has positive or negative significance for you. In simple terms, for example, we would probably consider thinking about losing your job as having a relatively negative frame of mind at the moment. If you have compelling reasons for thinking about it, and you find it important and profitable to do so, then you might still succeed in maintaining a relatively positive frame of mind. On the other hand, if you make a habit of worrying about all the disasters that could happen in your life, and you've found some obscure cause for worrying about keeping your job, then probably you've talked yourself into a negative frame of mind without good cause.

People vary widely in the ability to maintain a positive frame of mind by deliberate mental action. Some suffer with constant preoccupation about things going wrong, disaster, danger, failure, losing money, losing friends, getting mugged, having their car break down, and all the rest. Others acknowledge the possibility that those things can happen, but they choose to focus on the more positive and constructive items on their mental agendas.

Can you recall the last conversation you had with one or more acquaintances, in which the topic of discussion drifted into a negative or morbid orientation and took the entire conversation downward into a self-reinforcing negative spiral? Have you heard other people do this in ordinary social conversation? Without actually realizing it until much too late, people can drift from ordinary small talk or pleasant conversation into the most depressing subjects. By the time they snap out of it and realize what's happened, they have to shake off a negative frame of mind and get their feelings back to a positive level.

Perhaps you've inadvertently allowed some signal in your environment to trigger off an episode of musing about an unpleasant subject. A newspaper headline, radio announcement, bumper sticker, highway billboard, something someone says, unpleasant behavior by someone, all can provide you with signals that can hook you into a negative frame of mind for a while, if you allow them to. They invite you to descend into the self-reinforcing spiral of negative thoughts and negative feelings.

Just listening to the so-called news on radio or television can put almost anybody into a morbid frame of mind. Indeed, much of the typical programming material on television, and to a lesser extent in the movies, portrays the morbid, violent, hostile, dangerous, and sordid aspects of life far more extensively than the positive, affirmative, joyous aspects.

If you like to experiment, try turning off your television set for a full month; don't watch television at all during that period. For good measure, tune out the radio "news," skip over morbid and lurid accounts in magazines or newspapers, and conduct an active search for good news in the world. It might amaze you how positive the world of human beings really can seem, and how negative the "anxiety industry" makes it seem.

And if that kind of *input selection* process appeals to you, you'll probably find it a short step to other kinds of decisions about what you want to pay attention to. You might decide to associate more with some kinds of people and less with others. You might spend a little more time listening to pleasant music, reading interesting books and articles, and exploring interesting new ideas and activities. Turning off your television set can work wonders for your frame of mind, and it can make your life much more interesting as well.

We can state the input selection principle in this way: *protect the sanctity of your mind from all forms of emotional garbage.* Decide for yourself, on an active and continuing basis, what you will pay attention to and what subject matter you will entertain in your mind. Keep your thoughts positive and you keep your world positive.

As you become more familiar with this idea of input selection, and I hope more committed to it, begin to explore your environment with wide-open eyes. Sort through the various messages that surround you in the various settings you experience; identify those you consider positive and supportive, as well as those you consider negative and unconducive to a positive frame of mind. The more readily you can spot the various invitations to think and feel negatively, the more easily you can cancel their effects and eliminate them from your perceptual world. You can still deal with your life's issues and problems, but without unnecessary preoccupation with negative thoughts.

We can sum up these techniques for maintaining a positive frame of mind in terms of three specific processes:

1. *Self-monitoring*, or assessing your mood from moment to moment.
2. *Reframing your mind*, or simply "changing the subject" in your mind.
3. *Input selection*, or screening out unnecessary negative messages.

Once you accept responsibility for your frame of mind and begin to exercise the authority you have to control it, you won't accept outside influences that invite you to feel gloomy, discouraged, anxious, or angry. You can become the architect of your own mental world.

self-talk

Have you ever stopped to listen in on your personal, private monologue — the stream-of-consciousness commentary you make to yourself from moment to moment? This *self-talk*, the steady flow of things you say to yourself, usually silently but also aloud, plays a fundamental part in the way you organize your thoughts.

Think back for a moment and recall the most recent situation in which you felt thwarted, upset, defeated, or extremely frustrated. Recall a time when you made some blunder and became exasperated. Did you, at that time, get angry at yourself, criticize yourself, or call yourself unflattering names? To what extent did you verbalize an angry or hopeless outlook on the situation? To what extent did you verbalize a condemnatory picture of yourself?

Each person has a characteristic, habitual way of talking to himself as he goes about the everyday business of living. The stream of your self-talk includes statements you make to yourself *about* yourself, as well as about your experinces and the things going on in the world outside your head. Reflect for a moment on the overall orientation of your own particular stream of self-talk; then assess the extent to which it predisposes you toward a positive frame of mind or a negative one.

A person with a predominately negative self-estimate tends to use a largely negative form of self-talk and a style of self-description which condemns him in his own eyes before he even gives himself the chance to succeed. The person with a highly positive self-estimate tends toward a positive style of self-talk, which encodes his attitude of self-respect, self-acceptance, and expectation of success.

Within this concept of self-talk we can also include the idea of "implied" self-talk, or hypothetical staements which one might not have actually verbalized in his mind, but which he might just as well have said. Many people make extensive use of the implied self-talk statement "I can't do it." Others say, "I'm unattractive and unworthy of other people's attention." Others say, "I'm unlovable." In some cases, a person will say such things aloud, in so many words.

How often have you heard someone criticize himself, condemn himself, or describe himself as stupid, dumb, clumsy, inept, homely, fat, old, and so on? These kinds of statements affirm and reinforce a negative self-estimate. To what extent do you describe yourself in derogatory terms? As an experiment, listen carefully to yourself for a full day, taking note of any negative things you say about yourself. Do you find that you put yourself down routinely, in both subtle and obvious ways?

53

You can make your self-estimate much more positive simply by changing the way you talk to yourself. Begin by forbidding yourself ever to describe yourself in any of the following ways:

1. Any derogatory adjective, or "deradjective" (dumb, crazy, fat).
2. Any derogatory noun, or "doun" (nitwit, klutz, dingdong, failure).
3. Any categorical denial of your capability, your lovableness, or your worthiness as a person (I'm just no good at X, nobody would want an old bag like me, I'm just a loser).
4. Any categorical disaffirmation of your potential (I'll probably blow it, I'll never get anywhere).

Perhaps revising your style of self-talk so extensively seems like a tall order. Try it. You'll find that the more positively you speak to yourself and about yourself, the better you'll feel.

changing your language habits

We can easily extend the concept of positive self-talk to apply to virtually everything you say. By favoring terminology with a predominantly positive orientation, you continuously invite yourself to adopt a positive frame of mind. You also invite others to adopt a positive frame of mind and to keep their own moods highly positive.

Think of your total vocabulary for speaking, writing, and recognition as composed of three categories of terms. In one category, you have terms that have a highly *positive* connotation for you, such as happy, success, love, strong, home, peace, cooperate, and on and on to include thousands of them. You also know many terms in the *negative* category, such as hate, fear, disaster, violence, lose, crazy, and so on. And, of course, you have many *neutral* terms, such as numbers, names, articles of speech, and words that describe things and processes about which you have no particular reactions one way or the other. You can adopt the policy of deliberately excluding from your speaking, writing, and thinking processes those terms with a predominantly negative connotation, and reorganizing your statements using terms with positive connotations wherever possible. Monitor your use of language through a typical day. To what extent do you hear yourself using highly critical, negative, discouraging, or depressing terms? Do you describe your job as "driving me crazy"? Do you tell someone you feel tired by saying "I'm dead!"? Some people even use negatively oriented terminology to express ostensibly positive ideas. When asked how they feel, they reply "Not bad."

In a typical problem situation, try expressing the situation in terms of the future and in terms of what you want rather than of something having gone wrong. By consciously monitoring your language habits and by selectively revising them, you can create a strong and permanent orientation toward positive thoughts.

developing mental flexibility

Let's extend the idea of changing language habits one more step, and adopt a style of thinking, talking, and writing which conveys to others and reinforces in ourselves an overall orientation of mental flexibility. We can think of mental flexibility as the ability to adapt to new information, acknowledge various points of view in a situation, look for multiple causes and relationships, learn new things, entertain various options, and change one's mind when necessary.

Talking flexibly and adaptively requires you to think flexibly and adaptively. As you continue the process of monitoring your language habits, listen particularly for verbal constructions like rigid, "all-or-nothing" statements which convey dogmatic opinions, positions, or points of view. Listen for excessive or unqualified use of "allness" terms, such as always, everybody, nobody, never, and various absolutes and generalizations. To what extent do you identify your opinions and points of view as your own, and to what extent do you acknowledge the rights of others to think differently, rather than broadcasting flat categorical statements?

Listen also for excessive or unqualified use of "either-or" terms, which suggest only two polarized ways of thinking about a situation. These include word-pairs like win or lose, with us or against us, and right or wrong, as well as ways of describing problems in terms of only two completely contrasting alternatives. You might find it worthwhile to make more extensive use of qualifying terms and those that signal to others your willingness to hear new information or listen to new points of view. These include such terms as to me, so far as I know, from my point of view, in my opinion, up to a point, to a certain extent, and based on what I know right now.

You can maintain a high level of mental flexibility if you can freely and unapologetically say three things when situations call for them:

1. I don't know.
2. I made a mistake.
3. I changed my mind.

your happy switch

What if you could push a button whenever you discovered yourself in a down mood and instantly switch yourself to a happier mood? Imagine that you had such a push-button located on your chest, or in your bellybutton, or wherever you wanted it? Would you use it from time to time? Probably so. Well, you can actually create such a switch, by a simple technique involving visualization and memory.

If you'll grant the notion of mood level, or happiness level, as at least partially under your control, then probably you'll buy an approach to mood which treats it as a psychomotor skill. By doing something with your brain and nervous system, you can boost your mood level and increase your sense of personal power. The more often you do this, the more skilled at it you become.

You can install a "happy switch" in your body in the following way. Close your eyes, relax, and take your thoughts back to a recent situation which, for you, constituted a significant triumph. Visualize the situation in as much detail as possible, and allow the power feelings that came with it to well up strongly in yourself. Allow your body to revel in the sensation of power and the emotional high. Build the feeling as strongly as you can.

Now, retain the power feeling and detach it in your mind from the experience or event that "caused" it. Retain the mood and allow the specific situation-memory to fade away. Practice deliberately increasing the feeling and deliberately letting it subside. Now, as you allow the feeling to increase strongly, still with your eyes closed, simply snap your fingers briskly as you "print" the feeling into your kinesthetic memory. As you snap your fingers, form a vivid memory link between the finger snap and the power feeling. Practice this about a dozen times, each time snapping your fingers and simultaneously bringing back the power feeling. This simple trick will enable you to reach into you kinesthetic memory very quickly whenever you decide to do so, and you can call back the subjective sensation of a higher mood level. Practice this from time to time, and you'll find it quite easy to do.

You can use this happy switch in a variety of situations, whenever you want to feel better. Whenever you realize that you feel fatigued, hungry, or otherwise slightly out of sorts, you can quickly feel more cheerful. The happy switch probably won't get rid of your hunger, but it will help you to adapt to it more easily. After you've had a bit of bad news, you can return to a positive frame of mind quickly. You can also dispel negative thoughts and support your policy of input selection in the same way.

Try snapping your fingers in time to a cheerful piece of music and allowing it to put you into a cheerful mood. Or, make your own music as you walk along or go about your work.

56

If you find that you frequently need to boost your mood in situations that involve other people, you can select some unobtrusive memory trigger signal, which others would not see. For example, you could merely touch your thumb and index finger together, in the "OK" sign, and allow this to help you recall your power feelings.

If you've had significant difficulty with mood control in the past, you might find this technique surprisingly effective and very quick to accquire. See how soon you can arrive at a point where you feel cheerful and powerful more than ninety-five percent of the time.

dealing with frustration

How often do you feel frustrated? When? Under what circumstances? To what extent might you occasionally set yourself up for feeling frustrated? If you analyze the phenomenon of frustration and look at it in operational and behavioral terms, you might agree that you can prevent a great deal of your own frustration by adopting a strategic attitude about expectations and experiences.

Let's think through the phenomenon and the feeling. What, in a general sense, makes you feel frustrated? What features of the situation lead you to lose control of your mood and fly off the handle? Probably you feel frustrated when something that you want to happen fails to happen, and you can't control the situation as you would like to. The world has double crossed you. Someone refused to cooperate with you, or broke a promise. The person you planned to meet somewhere didn't show up. Someone pulled a dirty trick in traffic. You went to the shop to pick up your car, but they hadn't finished working on it, and they told you you'd have to wait until the next day to get it. The airplane didn't take off on time and you missed your connection. They lost your suitcase and told you it went either to Anchorage or Tampa, but they don't know which. You've lost some important papers and you can't go to the meeting without the data you need. And on and on. Life presents us with many of these double crosses. Sometimes reality unfolds according to our plans, and sometimes it doesn't.

We can define frustration as the emotional reaction you sometimes have after the world double crosses you. When you become frustrated, you've temporily gone crazy. You had formed a strong expectation, and you tried — irrationally — to cling to it in spite of the evidence that it wouldn't come true. These two key ingredients — a strongly held *exception* and a *double cross* by someone or something in your environment — form the basis for the feeling of frustration. Preventing or minimizing frustration amounts to accepting the reality that actually *has* happened, and adapting to it.

Have you ever heard yourself say, in some frustrating circumstance, "I can't believe it! I just can't *believe* it!"? When you say that, you probably mean "I won't accept it!" You've temporarily chosen to deny reality and to wallow in the angry and hostile feelings characteristic of frustration.

What happens next, after your "tantrum" subsides? Probably, sooner or later, you get over your indignant feeling, return to a problem-solving mode, make a more reasonable assessment of reality, accept it, and choose the most attractive course of action from among those left open to you. We can describe this flow of events as:

EXPECTATION → DOUBLE CROSS → FRUSTRATION → ADAPTATION

The sooner you accept the reality that confronts you, the sooner you can take a new adaptive action. In a sense, you have a choice about whether to feel frustrated and how long to keep feeling that way. You can assess your mood control skills partly in terms of the frequency and length of your tantrums. In the situation where you find out that they've lost your suitcase, you can get mad, throw a tantrum, accept the facts and adapt, or alternatively you can find out they've lost your suitcase and you can accept the facts and adapt. In the end, it comes to the same thing. In the first case, you've wasted some of your precious personal energy, and in the second case you've conserved it and gotten on with problem solving.

The very next time something happens that would normally frustrate you, stop for a few seconds and say, *out loud*, "I believe it." Affirm your perception of reality as quickly as possible. Then start thinking about what to do next. You'll probably find yourself getting frustrated much less often as you use this technique more and more. And when you do become angry over some double cross, deliberately make up your mind to keep your tantrum as short as possible. Get it over with in a reasonable period of time — a few seconds if possible — and get back to working on your higher level objectives.

changing your mood
by changing your posture

Have you considered the possibility that your body posture affects your mood, as well as the other way around? To verify this, you have but to conduct a small experiment. Sitting or standing, simply lean forward from the waist a bit, slump your shoulders far forward, look up at the ceiling, and let your jaw drop. You'll probably sense an immediate shift of your feelings, toward a childlike, inept, and subordinate subjective state.

Now adopt a contrasting posture. Stand or sit very tall, with your torso relaxed but erect. Bring your shoulders back, level your chin, and place your hands on your hips. You'll probably sense a markedly different subjective state, as if you feel "on top of things." This shift in mood level happens quite automatically, somewhere in the depths of your nervous system. Just as your frame of mind manifests itself in your body posture, your body posture can reorient your frame of mind.

The next time you feel out of sorts, slightly blue or irritable, fatigued, or listless, try dramatically changing your posture. Stand tall, square your shoulders, take a deep breath, and bring your entire body to the ready. Try this in situations where you might ordinarily feel fatigued, such as after a long airplane ride, after a particularly tense business meeting, or at the end of a hard day's work. See how quickly you can shift your mood by changing your posture. Learn to do this subtly and unobtrusively, and you'll have it available in virtually any situation you encounter.

SELF-ACTUALIZATION

the personal policy
of self-actualization

Psychologist Abraham Maslow usually gets credit for popularizing the term *self-actualization*. By this, Maslow meant a certain behavioral trend — a pattern of action in which you act freely according to your primary values most of the time in most situations, and in which you continue to learn, become more capable in various ways, and acquire and act on progressively "higher" values associated with enriching your mental life and appreciating esthetic experiences. Maslow liked to use terms like "growing" and "becoming" to describe this mode.

If we use the terms *self-actualization* and *self-actualizing* according to Maslow's original connotation, we can picture a behavioral *process* rather than some personal trait or static situation. From this point of view, we do not speak of a "self-actualized" person as if he or she has attained some end-point of personal development. Rather, we speak of a "self-actualizing" person as one who engages in the behavior of learning, developing, and acting upon primary values. This semantic difference can play a very important part in understanding personal effectiveness.

The competence category of self-actualization, then, includes various skills which we associate with the behavior pattern described above. For us, self-actualization means the behavior pattern of "actualizing" your primary values, that is, taking action to get those things or conditions in your life which you personally value, and it means engaging in behavior that leads you to learn, develop, and expand your capabilities. Each of us does this to some greater or lesser extent. Making self-actualization a conscious process requires clarifing your primary values and consciously evaluating your behavior and its consequences in your life.

living consciously

Most people live their lives inadvertently. Probably less than ten people out of 100 have really examined their lives, their behavior patterns, their reactions, their interactions with others, and the values that dominate their lives. Living effectively *means* living consciously. It means having a definite approach to one's life, based on the triad of personal effectiveness factors — authority, responsibility, and choice.

What does living consciously mean in specific behavioral terms? It means three things:

1. *Paying attention* to various key aspects of living.
2. *Analyzing* what you find out.
3. *Adapting* to what you find out.

The effectiveness with which you function in various aspects of your life depends in large measure on your skill at looking around you.

Psychologists identify an overall perceptual orientation, known as *field dependence*, in terms of the extent to which a person responds unconsciously to the variety of suggestive and directive messages present in his perceptual "field," or near environment. A highly field-dependent person tends to focus narrowly on the immediate matter at hand, without particularly scanning the situation and accounting for *contextual* influences and messages. He often tends, therefore, to fall prey to even the simplest manipulative or directive strategies employed by others who want to influence his behavior for their own purposes.

The field-independent person, on the other hand, tends to pay attention to a variety of aspects of a situation, both at the level of "context" and the level of "content." Without necessarily adopting a cynical orientation, the field-independent person stays alert for the ulterior, the manipulative, the biased interest or point of view, and the larger features of a situation that modify the obvious "meaning" which others derive from it. With respect to the ability to see through propaganda, phoney social values, manipulation, advertising, and other forms of social programming, Ernest Hemingway coined the charmingly blunt term "crap detecting." Hemingway once commented that a good writer needed "a built-in, shock-proof crap detector." We all need that.

With respect to the overall skill of paying attention, you might find it worthwhile to study your own attentional processes. As you go through a typical day, to what events and processes around you do you give your attention? What "blind spots" might you have about your own behavior? You might want to pay closer and more detailed attention to some of these areas:

1. The overall quality of your life, as you assess it for yourself.
2. Key "result areas" of your life, such as career, family, physical fitness, cultural activities, education, etc.
3. Your feelings and reactions in various situations.
4. The feelings and reactions of others.
5. Your language habits.
6. Your self-talk.
7. The actions of other people toward you.
8. The response of other people to your behavior — coworkers, family, mate or romantic partner, acquaintances, business contacts, etc.

9. The suggestive, directive, and persuasive messages coming to you from the people and the media in your environment; what they imply, hint at, or insinuate; what they don't say as well as what they say; the values, viewpoints, and stereotypes they convey and reinforce; the biases and special interests from which they approach you; the pressures, subtle and overt, which urge you to behave in certain ways.

As you review and assess the various goings-on around you and within you, you can develop a better understanding of the forces that tend to work against your own authority for managing your life, and you can formulate a more specific approach to actualizing your own values. By analyzing your interactions with your world, you can free yourself more and more from inadvertent processes, and you can behave more consciously to maximize the quality of life as you have defined it for yourself.

your "theoretical" values and your "operational" values

It has become popular for people to talk about their values, and about value systems, value judgements, and questions of value. This reflects, I think, a greater awareness of our three factors of authority, responsibility, and choice as basic components of personal effectiveness. We can make the discussion of personal values much more specific and operational if we adopt a behavioral point of view here too, just as we have with the other aspects of the subject.

Let's define a value as *a thing or a condition which you consistently act to get or to keep.* In this respect, the more consistently, persistently, and energetically you give your energies and resources to something, the more you apparently "value" it. This means that you can get a pretty clear idea of your values by conducting an inventory of your behavior.

Any attempt to make an exhaustive listing of possible values would probably get us lost in a forest of labels, but we can identify some overall categories which merit a close look. In thinking about your values, you might include job or career, money, material possessions, status, cars, clothes, personal appearance, friendships, marriage, sexuality and sexual activity, love relationships, work relationships, religion, exercise and physical fitness, eating habits, smoking, drinking, education, time alone, creative expression in a craft, music, or art form, cultural experiences, reading, abstract ideas or philosophies, travel, new experiences, sameness and routine in life, traditions and customs, and family relationships.

In each of these areas, as well as in the others you identify as worth thinking about, you can analyze your own behavior patterns and get an idea of how you presently seem to value them. You can also get a good clue to some of your operational values by noting the things you spend your money on. If, for example, you say you value education, ask yourself how much money you've spent on your education in the past five years or so. Although not the only measure, money does often serve as a useful barometer of your valuing processes.

Some people confuse and delude themselves with statements about their values. A person might say, "I want to get ahead in my job." Yet, if asked what he does, has done, and plans to do to get ahead, he or she might have trouble coming up with an answer. Talking about getting ahead has very little to do with getting ahead. It makes more sense to think of values as inferred by what the person *does*, not by what he or she *says*.

Probably each of us can identify similar disparities between our own talk and our action. You can think of your "theoretical" values as those things or conditions you say you want. You can think of your operational values as those things or conditions you actually do take action to get or keep. All of us have various unactualized theoretical values — things we want to do "some day." We have more possibilities than we'll ever have time to pursue. The most important measure of the self-actualizing mode, however, lies in the relative balance of theoretical and operational values, that is, the extent to which your behavior actualizes major values of your own choosing most of the time.

How many people do you know who can truthfully say that they live, at least for the most part, the way they really want to live? How many people go through their whole lives with their major desires unactualized, while they live up to the expectations, demands, and prescriptions of others? How many people drift with their circumstances, accepting less than life has to offer, and taking virtually no action to make their situations better?

The person with an underdeveloped level of competence in self-actualization has not adopted the executive attitude in his life. He has not fully assumed the *authority* to make *choices*, and he has not accepted the *responsibility* for consequences in his life. You can often hear the evidence of this limited sense of self-responsibility in what such a person says. The vocabulary of the chronically unhappy person tends to encode his general concept of himself as without authority, unentitled to choose according to his wants, and not responsible for negative results.

Often such a person will describe his life situation without significant reference to himself or to his behavior. He might say, "My life *is going* OK, I suppose." Or he might say, "*Things* are all screwed up. Nothing *is working* right." The absence of I-statements —

statements referring to one's self and describing one's own behavior — gives a significant clue to this person's tendency to try to transfer responsibility for his happiness to some outside agency.

Much of our verbal tradition encodes an attitude of passiveness, lack of control over our reactions and our happiness level, and helpless responsiveness to what others do. The frequently made statement "I *fell* in love" testifies to this trend. An old love song goes "You made me love you. I didn't want to do it." Another tune, a lament soliloquy, has the broken-hearted lover musing "Did I give enough? Did I give too much? Was I strong or was I weak? Did I talk too much?" and on and on. The singer really says, "I have no idea why she left me. Somehow, something went wrong, I guess I'm to blame, but I don't know why. What lousy luck." The song invites the singer and the hearer to adopt an attitude of martyrdom rather than responsible action.

The chronically unhappy lover doesn't understand that merely wanting something intensely — for example, the other person's constant presence, affection, and approval — doesn't make him entitled to it or guarantee that he'll eventually get it. If he doesn't change his unrealistic demands and expectations of the other person, he won't change his behavior in such a way as to get more desirable results. He tries unsuccessfully to actualize an unrealistic value. Only when you consciously acknowledge your authority and responsibility for your behavior can you actualize your most important wants and needs. By paying attention to the connections between your behavior and any unsuccessful consequences of it, you can change the behavior to get the consequences you want.

Make a habit of thinking over your personal values from time to time, identifying those you'd like to give more attention to and any others you want to change or stop "servicing." Write a list of some of the more important values in each of these categories. Any self-chosen behavior change you might want to undertake will only succeed to the extent that it brings you something you consciously value.

bringing your life into balance

To have balance in your life means getting worthwhile results in a variety of areas, all of which add up to your composite definition of quality of life. When you bring your life into balance, you don't wrap your whole life around one thing or one pursuit or one source of satisfaction. You develop a multiple reward system, which draws on many areas and which brings you a diversity of kinds of rewards.

fig. 7-1: thinking about key result areas helps you assess your "quality of life"

To use the management-by-objectives analogy, you can identify a half-dozen or so major *key result areas* of your life. A key result area amounts to a broad category you want to think about and which you consider indicative of your primary values. You can draw a pie diagram such as Figure 7-1, with each of a number of segments representing one of these key result areas. I suggest the following categories as a start:

Career/job/profession.
Financial.
Social.
Cultural.
Creative.
Personal.

You'll probably want to add others to suit your own specific purposes, such as family, religion, or certain highly specific categories. In the above list, the social category includes friendships, social activities, and virtually all important relationships with others. The cultural category deals with things you learn and experiences you have which enrich your understanding and appreciation of your society, other societies, and the world of people in general. Creative activities include anything that expresses you as a person, done for the pleasure of self-expression rather than for appreciation by anyone else. The personal area can include a variety of result conditions, such as physical fitness, overall health, physical appearance, personal habits, mental activity, self-education, spiritual pursuits, and self-development.

Many managers and professional people tend to focus their energies heavily in the career category, getting worthwhile results there, but often to the neglect of other areas which could also

66

greatly enrich their lives. The classic "workaholic" pattern revolves around a single source of satisfaction — the job — and allows the other areas to shrivel up and become relatively barren and unrewarding.

Once you have a clear definition of the principal result areas in your life, you can assess the results you actually get in each of them, and you can set some goals to make any improvements you choose. You might want to draw the pie diagram in the form of a "balance wheel," shading in each wedge to indicate your general level of satisfaction with that particular area right now. With high-satisfaction areas shaded out close to the rim and low-satisfaction areas shaded in with shorter radii, you can almost visualize the "out-of-round" condition you would like to correct.

Continuing the management-by-objectives analogy, you can set specific and realistic goals in any area you consider in need of development, or in all areas if you like. Then you can make practical plans for achieving those goals. This *process* of analyzing key result areas, deciding what changes to make, setting goals, making plans, and taking action to get the results you want, constitutes the behavior pattern of self-actualization as we have defined it.

some tips on goal-setting

Relatively few people really have well-defined, realistic, and rewarding goals set for themselves. Probably ninety out of 100 people live their lives more or less reactively, much as an amoeba drifts along without a plan. Most people seem to deal with events pretty much as they arise, with relatively little thought for the future, and relatively little of their present behavior aimed at bringing about long-term results. Each of us can profit from occasionally reviewing our goals, or if we have none then beginning to set some, and setting new ones as we achieve the others.

In setting goals, keep in mind these general rules:

1. Choose for your goals only those outcomes you would really value; make them worthwhile.
2. Start with many possibilities; make a want-list to choose from.
3. Start small at first; don't overdo it with too many undertakings; set a few readily achievable goals and develop the habit of working successfully to achieve them.
4. Set only those goals you feel you'll really work to achieve; avoid the "New Year's resolution" syndrome.

5. Set at least one goal in each key result area.

6. Give priority to the key result area most in need of development.

7. Use a mixture of short-range goals and long-range goals.

8. Subdivide long-term goals into manageable short-term goals.

9. Eliminate or revise fuzzy, vague, or overly general goal statements; make them specific, identifying concrete, observable things or conditions you will take as evidence you've achieved them.

10. Write down your goals; keep the plan brief, date it, and review it often.

self-renewal

An ancient philosopher said, "Age puts more wrinkles in the mind than in the face." Although I know of no law of nature that dictates that a person must become more rigid, narrow, attached to familiar ideas and ways of doing things, resistant to change and innovation, and unwilling to explore unfamiliar and unknown experiences, this seems to happen to the vast majority of human beings as they grow older. Probably ninety out of 100 people start becoming fossilized by about age thirty, and some people even before that. After they set their ideas, opinions, values, and preferences in concrete, they proceed to narrow down to the comfortable and reassuring routines they will probably follow for the rest of their lives.

Relatively few people maintain a conscious policy of *self-renewal*, continuing to learn new things, have new experiences, adapt to the changing times, and become more and more capable in various areas. Self-renewal and self-actualization go hand in hand. By continually actualizing your primary values, you continue to learn and grow, and you continue to have satisfying experiences which keep you psychologically young.

For the most part, a person decides for himself when — and whether — to get old. Some people start getting old at a very young chronological age, while others stay young and get younger for a very long time. Perhaps you've seen a person "go old" more or less suddenly, within a fairly short period. He will slow down physically and adopt more restricted and deliberate movements. He may begin stooping over more, and he may start to walk with a shuffle, or a slow trudging gait. He may make small noises of exertion when he sits or stands. He will probably begin to refer to himself as old; he will make jokes about getting too old to do this or that and about not having much longer to live. Some people go old in this way before age fifty, and others never do it.

Along with the physical signs come certain

psychological indicators. These include a loss of interest in new or unfamiliar things, a preoccupation with routine, comfort, and easily controllable patterns of living, less willingness to take risks, and frequent reminiscence about the past. It may also show up in a progressively rigid frame of mind, dominated by fixed opinions and categorical value judgments, lower tolerance for ambiguity or unresolved issues, and less willingness to revise one's viewpoints. Anthropologist Ashley Montagu refers to this condition as "psychosclerosis," otherwise known as "hardening of the categories." It signals a psychological aging process, not a physical one.

Just as a person can decide to go old, he can also decide to stay young — physically as well as psychologically. He can take good care of his health and fitness, and he can keep renewing his mental life to prevent wrinkles of the mind. The self-renewing, self-actualizing person deliberately organizes his life around learning experiences and opportunities to try new and different things. He consciously includes activities in his life which challenge and reward him, stimulate his ideas, and bring out capabilities he never knew he had. He consciously reflects on his primary values and keeps organizing and reorganizing his life so as to actualize those values as much as possible. He continues to analyze the key result areas of his life, set goals, make plans, and work to achieve them. He takes the responsibility for making his life interesting, and he acts to do so.

The British philosopher Joseph Addison observed, "Three things make for a happy life: Something to do, something to love, and something to hope for." We can translate this into challenging and satisfying work; positive relationships with others, including romantic relationships; and exciting plans for the future. When you have no future, you can consider yourself dead. So long as you have a future, you continue to live and to grow. Since you generally feel happiest when eagerly looking forward to something, it makes sense to always have something to look forward to. Keep planning, anticipating, doing, and renewing.

PRACTICAL ACTION

The third of our four competence categories, practical action, includes those skills which enable you to convert great thoughts into ordinary deeds. To actualize your values, to achieve your goals, and to establish an overall pattern of living that maximizes the quality of your life, you need a collection of well-developed skills for getting practical results. These include skills like organizing your personal environment, managing your time effectively, balancing priorities, solving problems and making effective decisions, changing habits, making practical and realistic plans, and converting your plans to day-to-day action. In this chapter, we explore a variety of these skills of practical action.

how to change your behavior

Mark Twain observed that "Habit is habit, and not to be thrown out the window by any man; but rather to be coaxed down the stairs one step at a time." This metaphor actually gives you all you need to know about changing your behavior. It constitutes a simple prescription which, unfortunately, very few people really appreciate and follow.

Most people seem to take it as an article of faith that "Habits are hard to break." And yet, very few people, apparently, have ever made a consistent, conscious, and well-planned attempt to change their habitual behavior. Most simply go right along in their well-learned, robotic behavior patterns, making no real attempt at analyzing them or changing them, and settling for a few hopeless New Year's resolutions so they can at least say they tried. But, in fact, if we take Mark Twain's prescription seriously, they haven't really tried.

To change your behavior, you must make a planned program of coaxing it down the stairs one step at a time. First, you have to specify the exact behavior pattern you want to adopt in place of the one you no longer want. Specify it in terms of *doing* something, rather than *not doing* something. For example, instead of "I want to stop losing my temper," you can say, "I want to stay calm and in control of the situation." Instead of "I want to stop smoking," say something like, "I want to keep my lungs clean and my body healthy." Whenever possible, set a goal toward which you can work as you change your behavior. This might include getting a certain promotion, saving at least a specified amount of money, reducing your weight by a certain amount, or exercising to some specified extent each week.

Rather than using various kinds of manipulative "white rat" techniques on yourself, you can change a habit fairly easily if you simply go about it with a plan, and if you first *want to change*.

Don't bother to try to change some behavior pattern unless you would really value the change. Change what you really want to change, and you'll find it rather simple to do. But how do you get yourself to "really" want to change, instead of just "theoretically" want to change?

You can change a habit most easily and reliably by first consciously *selling yourself* on the need for the change and the value of it. Just as you can arrange the facts and arguments to persuade someone else to buy a product, so you can arrange them to persuade yourself to buy the new habit. You can use the four-step AIDA model, which many salespeople use in keeping track of the flow of events while making a sale. The sequence of steps looks like this:

1. *Attention* — the buyer comes to realize the product (the new habit) exists; you keep reminding yourself of it.

2. *Interest* — the buyer wants to know more about the benefits and the specifics of the new product; you begin to really appreciate how life will get better.

3. *Desire* — the buyer really begins to want the product; you now really want to make the change because it will bring you something you value.

4. *Action* — the buyer pays the money or otherwise takes action to complete the deal; you begin behaving in the new way, at least part of the time.

If you've told yourself that you really want to do a certain thing, that is, behave in a certain way, and you still don't do it, then you must not have really "bought" the new behavior. You didn't really close the sale with yourself. For example, if you want to act more assertively in business situations, and you've picked out some specific behavior you want to make into a habit, then you first have to sell yourself as strongly as possible on the need to behave that way. You have to intensify your "advertising campaign" to yourself, by thinking over the benefits of the new behavior, frequently reminding yourself of it, removing or reducing obstacles to the new way, and getting strongly committed to the need for it. Place various cues and signals in your personal environment that serve as reminders. Once you've programmed your attitudes toward the new habit, you can easily program your behavior in that direction.

All along the way, you must keep the target behavior in your attention, noticing it from time to time, and reaffirming your intention to acquire it. Each time you behave in the new way, or a part of the new way, remind yourself of it and take credit for the improvement. Give yourself a mental "pat on the back" each time, and you'll soon find yourself developing a very positive feeling about the new pattern.

You'll probably find that you get better results by concentrating on one well-chosen habit at a time and working on it until you get it well programmed. As you go along, you may find that you can make other behavior changes more easily and in less time. Probably, a person develops a bit of skill at actually changing behavior, and this skill applies in a general way to many ordinary patterns. In any case, choose your first project carefully, to maximize the chances of success using the AIDA model.

You might choose to change behavior patterns such as:

Overeating.

Smoking.

Drinking too much alcohol.

Drinking too much coffee or other stimulants.

Talking too much.

Interrupting others.

Not talking enough.

Arriving late to scheduled activities or appointments.

Having things around you disorganized.

Getting insufficient exercise or physical activity.

In each case, start by converting the problem area into a specific, positively stated target behavior which you can observe in yourself and which has value for you. Change "talking too much" to "letting others talk more than fifty percent of the time," and so on. Then begin to concentrate on behaving in that way, and you'll prettty quickly substitute the new habit for the undesirable one.

"I don't have time": the activity trap

For most people, the matter of time probably presents the most difficult obstacle to getting high-value results in the variety of areas that make up the total quality of life. Most of us seem to have too much to do and too little time available. *Time competence* means the ability to use time strategically to get the maximum in the way of worthwhile results.

Time-incompetent people usually fall into the *activity trap* and stay there. In the activity trap, either on the job or in private life, a person finds his day filled up with things he "has to do," and he forever lags behind. The activity trap goes hand in hand with the "amoebic" behavior pattern, a drifting, goalless mode in which he deals with whatever matter — urgent or trivial — demands his attention next. At the end of a week, or a month, or a year, or a lifetime, he has accomplished many insignificant things and few really significant things. This happens because the important, high-payoff items came along in line just like the horde of routine items. He allowed the trivial many to overwhelm the significant few. The time-incompetent person usually can't find time to do many of the things he would like to do, simply because he can't detach himself from the "tar baby" of everyday routines and trivial crises. With the statement "I don't have time," he signals an "irresponsible" attitude about results.

The time-competent person, on the other hand, lives and works with a strategic attitude about time, an executive attitude about consciously choosing what to do and what to defer, and a systematic way of assigning priorities to the various demands on his time, based on overall payoff. He uses the skills and techniques of *time management*. He deliberately manages his situation, rather than allowing it to manage him.

managing your time

The skill of time management applies just as well to private activities as to work activities, so we will deal with both of them in this section. Managing time, in specific behavioral terms, means the following:

1. Itemizing all significant things you feel you must accomplish, and writing them down on a current list of things to do.

2. Evaluating each item in terms of its overall importance, judged by the total payoff it will bring; comparing the items in terms of payoff and assigning relative priorities to them.

3. Proceeding to get them done by working in a pattern that ensures that, over the long run, you will aggressively favor those items with the highest payoff.

4. Using various time-structuring techniques to maximize the efficiency of your activities, minimize wasted time, resist unwarranted encroachments on your time, and keep your overall objectives in view.

Your only hope for gaining control of your time lies in *using* — not just having — a written list of things to do, as a thinking tool, a management tool, and a day-to-day basis for making choices about how to spend your time. If you don't presently use a "to-do" list, I recommend you try it for a period of two full weeks, to get the hang of writing down items as they occur to you, crossing off those you've completed, and reviewing status frequently.

Next, you need a priority system. Try using the old "80/20 rule," which says that only about 20 percent of the things on your list really warrant high-priority attention, because they probably account for about 80 percent of your total payoff. The other 80 percent of the items, if lumped together, probably bring the other 20 percent of the payoff. This means that you can prioritize your things to do in terms of a small category of high-priority items and a larger second category of "all the rest." If you like, you can also break down the second category into a second and third level of priority, say 30 percent and 50 percent. Thus, the total "pie" of things you've chosen to get done will have three levels, such as A, B, and C, as illustrated by Figure 8–1.

In using this approach, count the items on your list (say twenty-five) and take 20 percent of that number (five) as the maximum number of items you will designate as priority A. After you flag those particular items on the list, let the others fall into line behind them. In setting priority levels, you have to account for a variety of factors, including, for example, what your boss considers important, any time urgency involved, possible penalties associated with not getting something done, the direct significance it has for you, and so on. This

fig. 8-1: choosing a small number of things to do as top priority enables you to focus your efforts for maximum payoff

THINGS TO DO THIS WEEK	PRIORITY (Circle One)	NOTES
1.	A B C	
2.	A B C	
3.	A B C	
4.	A B C	
5.	A B C	
6.	A B C	
7.	A B C	
8.	A B C	
9.	A B C	
10.	A B C	
11.	A B C	
12.	A B C	
13.	A B C	
14.	A B C	
15.	A B C	
16.	A B C	
17.	A B C	
18.	A B C	
19.	A B C	
20.	A B C	
21.	A B C	
22.	A B C	
23.	A B C	
24.	A B C	
25.	A B C	

constitutes your assessment of the total payoff for any one item. You can easily see the necessity of itemizing them all on a written list in order to make choices. You might choose to include personal matters as well as work items on the same time-management list, since they both involve the allocation of your time.

Next comes the policy of working aggressively to maximize payoff. This means that, as you make choices about how to spend your time at various points throughout a typical day, you refer to your to-do list and choose the item that most needs doing at that particular time. Within your long-term policy of favoring priority-A items, you can use various opportunities to get lower priority items done as well, provided you keep your attention on payoff as a general matter.

Try making yourself a worksheet such as Figure 8–2. Keep it in your daily planner or calendar and refer to it occasionally throughout the day. Cross off items as you get them done, a habit which will also give you a continuing sense of accomplishment. As you add any new item, give it a priority rating and consider its importance with respect to the others.

Time management involves maximizing accomplishment, not saving and conserving time. If you shift your point of view in this way, you can see that using a prioritized to-do list maximizes your freedom of choice, an essential element of the executive attitude of personal effectiveness. This foundation of effective use of your time enables you to use various time-structuring techniques which can then increase your efficiency in various activities.

For example, you can usually schedule your various activities to some extent, favoring certain kinds of tasks for "prime time," when you feel alert, refreshed, and able to concentrate

fig. 8-2: a time-management worksheet can help you keep track of priorities and accomplishments

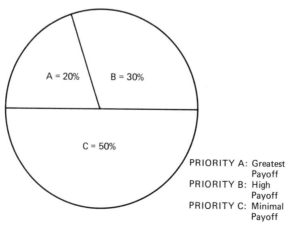

A = 20%   B = 30%

C = 50%

PRIORITY A: Greatest Payoff
PRIORITY B: High Payoff
PRIORITY C: Minimal Payoff

well. Others might go better if you do them during in-between times, such as riding on an airplane, waiting in someone's office, or while taking care of some other related matter. You can eliminate those activities that waste your time without returning worthwhile results. You can focus your business reading to cover only items of high value to you, rather than wading through everything. You don't have to read every memo, every announcement, and every report that floats across your desk. Cut off some of this verbal garbage at its source, and improve the content level of your information stream.

You can minimize the time you spend with routine paperwork by handling each item only once, if possible. If something merely requires your quick review and signature, stop for a few seconds and dispose of it. By putting it on a pile of things to take care of later, you handle it twice, and probably for twice as long. You can also decide what not to do. Some "urgent" problems merely go away if ignored. You can simply refuse to get involved with trivia.

If you deal with others frequently, you might want to review your habits in this area and minimize the extent to which you permit others to encroach upon your time. Although you must accept certain interruptions and impositions, you might find that you permit some of them unnecessarily. If you manage others, you might want to delegate more extensively, assign tasks in whole "packages," and limit casual interruptions by your employees. Just make sure you don't overdo it; don't go to the extreme of making yourself unavailable to staff members when they need your help.

In your private life, time management provides a key to reorganizing your activities as you see fit and maximizing quality of life by bringing your key result areas into balance. First, forbid yourself to say "I don't have time to . . ." when you talk about the various discretionary activities open to you. "I don't have time to exercise" really means "I don't consider exercise important enough to allocate time to it." At least accept responsibility for the decision you made about exercise. If you want to change that decision, you merely have to make time for exercise. Time-management skills enable you to do this. Changing such a decision probably involves more of a change in your views about exercise than a change in your activities. Everybody gets the same twenty-four hours each day, and each of us uses those hours according to choices we make or have made. We can remake those choices if we want to.

If you watch television extensively — more than an hour a day — you can probably find plenty of time for new activities and for taking action on the goals you want to set for yourself. When payoffs in the other areas become more attractive to you than sitting passively in front of the set and having your brain homogenized, you'll reallocate your time to them.

By combining the techniques of clarifying

your values, making choices, changing habits, setting goals, and taking action with the techniques of managing time, you free yourself to live as you choose.

problem solving
and decision making

The comprehensive skill of solving problems plays a very important part in a person's practical-action capability. People seem to vary widely in their ability to identify, isolate, analyze, and resolve problem issues in their lives, careers, and jobs. The ineffective individual usually lacks this kind of competence to a significant extent. The highly effective individual has acquired it in good measure and uses it routinely.

For our purposes, let's define a problem broadly, as *a state of affairs you have to change in order to get what you want.* This removes any particular connotation of something having "gone wrong," and it includes those situations in which you simply want to improve on something or add something by initiative. Decision making simply constitutes one step in the process of problem solving.

An incompetent problem-solver might display some of the following behaviors:

1. Chronic "decidophobia"; vacillating, postponing decisions, waiting, finding excuses to justify not deciding and taking action.

2. Trying to get others to make decisions for him; trying to shift responsibility for decisions, large and small, to other people.

3. Drifting with unresolved personal or interpersonal problems; accepting less than he wants while refusing to face the issues.

4. Snap-deciding; going off half-cocked with insufficient information, insufficient thought, and inadequate preparation for action.

5. Confusing emotional factors with factual factors; allowing guilt, jealousy, or the expectations of others to bias judgements.

6. Deciding reactively rather than anticipatorily; dealing with problems only when they present themselves.

7. Choosing from too small a range of options, including having only one "standard" way of doing things; failing to consider the range of possibilities inherent in a problem situation.

The competent problem-solver usually displays the following behaviors:

1. Facing problems and issues squarely and honestly; acknowledging them and going to work on them.

2. Anticipating significant problems and issues; getting a head start on them by thinking about them, gathering information, and preparing to solve them.

3. Waiting for a problem to "ripen," that is, choosing the appropriate time for dealing with it, rather than jumping the gun.

4. Thinking problems through; considering a wide variety of factors, such as the roles and interests of others, hidden assumptions or values imbedded in the way someone else has described the problem, significant constraints or requirements, and overall objectives.

5. Attacking a problem in stages; clarifying it first, identifying the end condition he wants to achieve, then generating as many reasonable options as possible for solving it, studying the options, selecting the most promising one, making a plan, and carrying it through to action.

6. Following through on solutions to make sure that the problem really got solved; approaching the problem with a "closed-loop," problem-solving process, in which he compares the results actually achieved with the results intended, and repeats the process if necessary.

You might find it helpful to consciously apply a stepwise thinking process in dealing with many of your issues, a kind of recipe which serves as a conceptual basis for virtually all problem solving. You can think of your problem-solving process as proceeding in roughly the following steps:

1. *Problem finding* — seeing a problem coming, identifying some present condition that needs changing, searching for significant issues, and anticipating the need for action in some area.

2. *Problem stating* — clarifying the problem; expressing it in various ways and from various points of view; enlarging it and including extra factors you might have otherwise overlooked; inventorying the key issues; breaking it down into smaller component problems if appropriate; identifying end conditions that will constitute a solution.

3. *Option finding* — coming up with as many reasonable possibilities as you can for solving it.

4. *Deciding* — comparing the various options in some consistent way and choosing the option or combination of options you consider best.

5. *Taking action* — putting your solution into play, with a practical approach aimed at getting the desired results as efficiently as possible.

6. *Evaluating results* — comparing results with intentions; identifying shortfalls, or areas in which your action hasn't completely achieved the desired results; figuring out what you have to do to make it work.

The step of evaluating results becomes the starting point for another cycle of the process, that is, problem finding, if you haven't yet achieved the results you want.

You can build your overall problem-solving skills by consciously using a stepwise problem-solving model such as this when dealing with significant issues. You probably don't need such an extensive thought process to figure out where to go for lunch, but you can indeed benefit from it when you attack the problem of reducing your weight by twenty pounds. You can also increase your problem-solving competence by developing a few other useful habits.

For example, you can become more problem conscious by paying closer attention to problems as they arise and thinking about them as problems in themselves, which can challenge and develop your problem-solving capabilities. If you make a habit of talking about problems and decisions, and talking in terms of the various stages of the problem-solving model, you will add an extra level to your thinking.

Keep a *problem list* or a *decision list* in your calender, possibly clipped to your time-management worksheet. From time to time, reflect on upcoming situations or events that might present you with problems to solve or decisions to make. Start working on these items well in advance of the time when they ripen. Use a pen and paper to attack a selected problem, logically and systematically.

If you find that you have too many problems, issues, concerns, and threatening situations orbiting around your head at one time, use a *worry list* to get them pinned down. Give each of them a descriptive label and write it down. When you've itemized all of the most troublesome problems you face, you can isolate them and begin attacking them one at a time.

Form the *option-thinking* habit. Train yourself to look for options, for the nonobvious alternative, the novel approach, the way to do it that might solve several problems at once. Use your divergent, imaginative, productive thinking processes to come up with new and novel ways to do things. Try keeping an *idea list* clipped to your time-management worksheet, too. Write down your ideas as they come to you. Capture and save them, even if they appeal only to you. When you don't have your idea list with you, jot your ideas down on paper napkins, paper placemats, the backs of business cards, or anything else available, so you can recall them later and put them on the list. You may find that this habit tends to increase your idea-production skills, making you much more effective as an innovator and a practical problem-solver.*

getting organized

How well organized do you consider yourself? What viewpoint do you have about the matter of personal organization? Some people have so little organization in their lives that they continually flounder about, seldom ever doing anything effectively or efficiently for lack of some item of information, a physical article, a tool, or a needed material. Others go to the extreme, compulsively arranging, cataloguing, labeling, filing, and storing things, without necessarily increasing their ability to do practical things effectively. In general, underorganized people seem to outnumber overorganized people by a wide margin. Let's consider the factors involved in a working definition of "appropriately organized."

In my opinion, an appropriately organized person has a clear concept of his personal environment, both at work and at home, and sees it as consisting of useful things and useful information. He has acquired a variety of personal resources to help him do what he wants to do. And he has arranged his personal environment so that he can usually find something he needs quickly and with minimum disruption. By this definition, many people fail miserably. Some people can't even locate a postage stamp on an hour's notice. Other people have generally mastered the practical aspects of organizing and finding things, and they can usually draw upon their resources effectively.

Even the most underorganized person can take some straightforward actions to gain a greater measure of control over his personal environment. If you consider yourself somewhat under-organized, you can approach the process of getting appropriately organized systematically and in manageable steps. First, make an inventory of your personal resources, in the form of two lists. On one list, itemize the *physical* belongings you have which you consider useful. These might include your car, your bicycle, your clothing, your household furnishings, your tools, your hobby materials or resources, your musical instruments, records, tapes, your desk, any office equipment and materi-

*For additional information on problem solving and decision making, read *Brain Power* by Karl Albrecht (Englewood Cliffs, N.J.: Prentice-Hall, Inc., 1980). Providing illustrations, games, and puzzles to stimulate brain power, this book helps people sharpen their thinking skills and shows how to use creative problem-solving strategies in the business world. Specific techniques for maintaining a positive frame of mind while blocking out negative feelings are also provided.

als you may own, and so on. Your *informational* resources might include your personal history records, medical data, bills and receipts, sheet music, books, magazine articles you've clipped, photographs, negatives, slides, reference materials such as dictionaries, almanacs, encyclopedias, and so on.

When you have a reasonably complete list, review the various items with one question in mind: how easily could you find some particular item if you wanted it? Indeed, do you really know what you have? Do you have countless boxes of things tucked into various nooks and crannies? Have you surrounded yourself with junk which you no longer use or need? Would you have to wade through it in order to find something of value? If you wanted to find a particular photograph from five or ten years ago, would it take a concerted research effort of several hours, or could you go to a file of photographs and negatives and find it within a few minutes? Can you find a bank statement from a year ago without having to rummage through a shoe box full of garbage? If you needed some important fact or other bit of information, could you generally come up with it within fifteen minutes or so? Merely knowing where to locate a pile of garbage that probably contains the item of interest doesn't qualify as having organized things, by this definition. You need the ability to find a fairly specific item fairly quickly, most of the time.

Having made such an inventory, you can then identify the things in your personal resource base that you'd like to organize more effectively. Don't try to attack the entire thing in one heroic episode. Instead, subdivide the job into a series of smaller projects, each of which you can complete with a reasonably small investment of effort and time. For example, as one project you might decide to organize all of your photographs and negatives. At work, you might decide to reorganize and simplify your records for dealing with a certain area of responsibility. You might have a large number of technical articles or clippings of interest to you, which you'd like to arrange in such a way as to make it easy to find one of them when you want it. Once you have a complete list of individual projects, pick out the one you want to attack first, then go to it.

Additional suggestions for getting appropriately organized include:

1. Don't drown yourself in physical possessions, especially wasteful consumer trivia and small gadgetry; ruthlessly throw out junk; give away things you don't need to charitable agencies; reduce your belongings to those items you really value.

2. Don't "save string"; unless you have a very probable need for some random item, even though it "seems" useful, get rid of it.

3. Set up a convenient, well-supplied, and

well-organized personal office; get a desk and any other office equipment you find useful; invest in a good file cabinet; stock your office with plenty of paper, pens, pencils, paper clips, rubber bands, stamps, and everything else that makes it easy for you to sit down and take care of some item of action; make it a comfortable and supportive place to work; don't clutter it with other unrelated things.

4. Create a comfortable degree of physical order all around you; decide how neat you want to make your personal environment; keep the work involved in organizing it appropriate to its relative importance to you.

5. Build and maintain a personal database; this includes your library, files, references, personal records, photographs, music, notes of various kinds, and any other useful data you want to organize and keep available.

6. Consider using looseleaf notebooks to organize your database; buy plenty of them and a three-hole punch; file various clippings and articles in logical categories, one category per notebook. Instead of having your bills and bank statements stuffed into shoeboxes, flatten them out, throw away the envelopes, punch them, put them in chronological order, and file them in a large notebook; use looseleaf dividers liberally; purge your file system frequently and ruthlessly.

7. Form the habit of writing dates on things as you put them away; it helps in reading some note or other item to know when you found it; when someone gives you his or her business card, write the date on the back, and possibly a word or two to let you know where you met the person.

8. Consciously design and arrange your information stream; choose magazines or other publications you consider important or useful to you; eliminate marginal ones; get into the habit of exchanging books and copies of interesting articles with friends and colleagues; keep one another informed.

9. Cut your reading time drastically and make it more productive by using a reading file; when a magazine arrives, for example, spend five minutes tearing out only those articles you consider highly worthwhile reading, and throw out the carcass; put the articles in a file folder, arranged in order for priority reading; pass up the "nice to read" articles (which you probably wouldn't get around to reading anyway) and don't wade through all the advertisements; throw away most of the articles after you've read them, except the few you decide to keep and file in looseleaf notebooks; throw away any unread magazine older than three months.

10. Keep a personal planning notebook, with a divider for each of the key result areas you established as a result of the thinking process described in Chapter 7. Browse through it from time to time, making notes and adding ideas; keep it simple, brief, and useful.

MANAGING STRESS AND DEVELOPING WELLNESS

your physical capital

Thanks to the automobile, the television set, and the advertising industry, Americans have become the most sedentary people of any nation in the world. Until quite recently, exercising to any extent greater than a week-end golf game had the stigma of fanaticism. Somehow, we "evolved" to the point where anybody who exercised frequently, refused to dine regularly on Big Macs, Cokes, and french fries, didn't smoke cigarettes, and didn't drink liquor much or at all earned for himself or herself the label of "health nut." In the space of less than one generation, Americans as a group went from a robust, trim, hard-working, active people to a nation of self-indulgent, sedentary slobs. With the simultaneous decline in the incidence of infectious diseases and the rise of the much-touted "American good life," Americans became both healthier and less "well" — in the broadest sense — than ever before.

As self-actualizing professional people, we must now acknowledge the crucial significance of managing our "physical capital" — our precious health. Returning to the analogy of your life as a kind of enterprise, similiar to a company, and with you yourself functioning as the chief executive, we can compare your body to the physical plant of the company. Just as a company has a share of its total assets invested in the buildings, equipment, and facilities, you also have a tremendous share of your own resources tied up in your physical self. When your body goes, you go.

Most of us go through our early adult years shamefully neglecting, ignoring, and sometimes even abusing our bodies, probably because a young body can withstand an incredible amount of abuse and still bounce back. When the body works well, has a high energy level, and continually restores itself, its owner has very little need to pay attention to it. But think about the times when you got sick, injured, or otherwise found yourself severely limited physically. At those times it probably came home to you quite clearly how much you depended on feeling good in order to function effectively in your life. People with severe disabilities or chronic incapacitating illnesses know this all too well. The rest of us tend to take our good fortune for granted.

Probably the vast majority of Americans follow roughly the same downhill trajectory in physical fitness, increasing body weight, and indulgent habits of eating and drinking, after they leave their parents' homes, finish their basic education, and go out on their own to get jobs and set up households. We can almost define a characteristic syndrome of health behavior and appearance, which deserves the label of the "Standard American Middle-Class Slob." Although a number of people continue to take good care of themselves and stay in good condition all their lives, probably two-thirds or more of adult Americans fall far short of a reasonable standard in maintaining their physical capital.

85

the standard american middle-aged physique

How does this syndrome come about? How does a trim, physically fit, active, good-looking young man turn into a forty-year-old slob? How does a pretty, shapely, fit, vivacious young lady turn into a forty-year-old bag? Very simply: one day at a time.

Because most people pay so little attention to their physical capital during the years when it serves them well, and because the American environment surrounding them invites them to "take it easy," a large number of people drift steadily into the same minimally active pattern of living, giving most of their attention to getting ahead in the abstract world of career, money, and material possessions.

This has now begun to change. More and more professional people, of all ages, have started to return to a serious interest in fitness and well-being. This trend will probably continue and increase to much larger proportions.

wellness vs. "health"

We need to revise our viewpoint about human physical capital. The word *health* has become obsolete, in the sense that we have used it for many years and in the sense that physicians use it. Americans have come to accept such a low level of physical functioning as "health" that most of them apparently don't know how really good a person can feel most of the time.

Many people don't seem to realize it, but the medical definition of health falls considerably short of the conditions required to feel good. To the physician, health means *the absence of any symptoms that would suggest the existence of an underlying organic disorder.* This means you can go to a traditionally oriented physician with frequent headaches, indigestion, constipation or diarrhea, muscle cramps, insomnia, or chronic fatigue and have him or her pronounce you healthy. You may feel lousy, but from the point of view of contemporary medical practice, the physician considers you basically healthy. Carleton Fredericks, the noted nutritionist, said, "To the typical doctor, good health means the ability to remain upright in a strong wind."

A small and growing number of physicians have begun to emphasize the broader context of health as a matter of a well-managed life-style, with effective use of exercise, diet, and emotional health strategies, to produce a condition of high-level "wellness." The term *wellness* implies a more comprehensive view of human physical functioning and offers a clear-cut avenue for adult professional people to take action and make improvements.

stress: what it does to you and how to manage it

The topic of *stress* has received a great deal of attention in recent years, and rightly so. Medical researchers, most notably Dr. Hans Selye at the University of Montreal, have helped us to understand the stress syndrome as the body's characteristic response to the demands of living and adapting, both physically and emotionally. We've begun to get a clearer idea of what chronic overstress does to the human body and the extent to which it aggravates, contributes to, and in some cases causes degenerative disease.

Medical people define stress as a *characteristic pattern of nervous system activity and hormone flows in the body, which manifests the level of intensity of its functioning.* Selye defines it in layman's terms as *the rate of wear and tear on the body caused by living.* Your stress level, in the form of the relative tempo of your organ processes, prepares your body to meet whatever physical or emotional challenges you currently perceive and react to. Emotional arousal, significant disease or injury, and physical exertion all increase your stress level, automatically enabling you to deal effectively with the situation. Your stress level fluctuates from moment to moment throughout your waking hours and settles down to a comparative minimum while you sleep

— if you sleep peacefully. You can consider your instantaneous stress level a barometer of your body's functioning.

The importance of stress as a contemporary subject probably warrants your reading a good book devoted entirely to the subject.* For this discussion let's clear up several of the most common misconceptions and identify a few useful strategies. The more common misconceptions about stress include:

1. "Stress is a general term for the pressures and problems of living." The medical definition of stress, as we've seen, treats it as a highly specific phenomenon; don't confuse *pressure* — an aspect of the outside world, to which you can choose to react in various ways — with *stress* — an aspect of your interior, biological world, which stems from your reaction to the pressure.

2. "Stress is bad for you." Let's think of stress as neither good nor bad, but merely as a normal aspect of your body's functioning.

3. "You should try to eliminate stress from your life." To do that, you'd have to die. Only dead people have no stress; the rest of us, no matter how relaxed or inert we become, always have at least some minimal stress level as a part of our functioning organic processes.

4. "Negative experiences and reactions cause high stress." Actually, your stress level goes up naturally as a result of highly positive experiences, just as it does for highly negative experiences; from your hypothalamus on down, your body can't tell the difference, for example, between getting fired from your job and getting married (taking those as examples of presumed negative and positive experiences, respectively).

5. "Stress can ruin your health, cause degenerative diseases like ulcer, heart attack, and stroke, and it can even kill you." Only *overstress* can have these effects, and only prolonged *chronic* overstress at that. By managing your life so as to keep your stress level within your personal *comfort zone* most of the time, while deriving a sense of accomplishment at whatever you do, you can stay healthy and well for a very long time.

Stress-management skills include self-monitoring, or "reading" your body's stress level from time to time, various mood-control techniques such as those described in Chapter 6, en-

---

Stress and the Manager: Making It Work for You by Karl Albrecht (Englewood Cliffs, N.J.: Prentice-Hall, Inc., 1979) explains how business people can utilize problem-solving resources to reduce environmental and professional stress — to save time, money, and emotional turmoil.

gineering your work and life activities to maximize reward while keeping your stress level within your comfort zone, and the psychomotor skill of deep relaxation.

Most effective training seminars in stress management include various techniques for self-induced deep relaxation, a state of your body in which your stress level drops dramatically, your muscles become profoundly relaxed, and your organ processes slow down. This state seems to have the effect of profoundly resting your body, even more than sleeping does, and it seems to more or less rebalance your overall nervous system and increase your reactive tolerance to various situations. This means that you can deal with pressure situations more effectively, while having your stress level remain within your comfort zone more of the time. Training techniques such as progressive muscle relaxation, meditation, self-hypnosis, autogenic training, and biofeedback can help you to acquire this deep relaxation skill. You can treat yourself to a fifteen- or twenty-minute period of relaxation each day. You can also use a momentary relaxation technique in conjunction with the self-monitoring technique to pause occasionally and "de-escalate" your internal level, returning to a more comfortable state of relaxed but alert functioning.

You can think of your total stress "score" over a period of time as the price you pay in body energy and wear and tear, in exchange for the rewards you get out of your various activities. Conversely, you can think of the quality of your life and your long-term rewards as returns on invested stress energy. This "return-on-investment" (ROI) notion continues the analogy we've used previously, of your life as an enterprise which you consciously manage. You can maximize ROI and live with your stress level quite happily if you organize, balance, and manage your life consciously and effectively.

the wellness triad

Three specific factors recur frequently in the study of general wellness. These factors, taken together, seem to work synergistically or antisynergistically, according to how much a person tends to them. In terms of "wellness behavior," you tend to keep yourself well to the extent that you take effective action in each of these categories:

1. *Relaxation* — the extent to which you use some of your time to detach from the swirl of activity around you, become quiet, relax your body, and let it rest and restore its processes; this means more than just sleeping regularly; it includes waking relaxation, quiet recreation, and peaceful detachment.

2. *Exercise* — particularly *aerobic* exercise, defined as activity that increases your heart rate and oxygen consumption to an established target level and keeps it there for a reasonable period of time, bringing about an increase in cardiovascular efficiency and lung function, as well as a profound rejuvenation of all your organs.

3. *Diet* — the sum of everything you take into your body, with the definition extended to include items like nicotine, caffeine, and other stimulants, as well as alcohol and various other recreational chemicals.

By paying fairly careful attention to each of these factors, a person needn't become fanatical about any of them, because they combine to promote a relatively high level of wellness. You don't have to retreat to a monastery and spend your time meditating; you don't have to adhere to an ascetic macrobiotic diet; and you don't have to run the marathon. You can do any or all of these if you choose, but if you adopt a reasonable and consistent approach to all three of the key categories, you can readily achieve a level of wellness higher than about ninety-five percent of your fellow citizens.

I refer to these three factors taken together — relaxation, exercise, and diet — as the *wellness triad*, or R.E.D. triad, after the acronym they suggest. By keeping the acronym in mind and using it as a wellness behavior criterion, you can manage your physical capital effectively with a reasonable amount of time and effort.

getting back into shape

For most Americans, the idea of regular exercise of any kind seems to have the distinct connotation of self-punishment and suffering. Sedentary people tend to dread the whole idea of exercise, and so they tend to block it out of their thinking and planning processes. They also tend to develop rationalizations which allow them to dismiss it as relatively unimportant. Most males, in particular, seem to have distorted ideas about strenuous exercise and the need to demonstrate "manliness" by extreme physical effort. In military life, exercise often serves as a form of punishment for minor disciplinary infractions. Few men have any idea how to exercise sensibly and without overexerting themselves.

These experiences, and prevailing American values about exercise, tend to discourage a typical adult professional person who nevertheless understands, at least vaguely, the importance of keeping his or her body active and reasonably fit. If you find yourself somewhat out of shape, or very out of shape, and you'd like to get back into good condition, you can do so fairly easily, and indeed even enjoyably, if you adopt a strategic approach to making exercise a positive habit.

The following strategy for getting back into shape applies in various forms to virtually any personal change you want to make, including reducing your weight. It rests on two basic policies, both of which you must understand and really appreciate in order to apply it. I refer to these two interrelated policies as *gradualism* and *nonpunishment*. Both of them involve trading off time for comfortable and enjoyable progress. By proceeding at a rate which keeps you physically in your comfort zone, you can stay with an exercise program indefinitely, seeing gradual but continuous improvement. In order to understand the importance of gradualism and nonpunishment, let's review the typical "getting into shape syndrome" which so many of us have tried and given up on. The following description applies just about as much to women as to men, even though it uses the general pronoun *he* for descriptive convenience.

Typically, a person will start feeling guilty about having gotten so far out of shape and having taken such poor care of his body. So he decides to start exercising. Jogging sounds like a good idea. So, the very next morning, before going to work, he gets up at the crack of dawn and goes out to the beach, the park, or the local high school track and starts running. Not having even run to catch a bus for months or possibly even years, he quickly overexerts himself. He finishes up a mile — much too long a distance for an out-of-shape person — feeling nearly exhausted, but concluding "it hurts like hell, so it must be good for me." All of his erroneous personal traditions tell him that in order to get into shape, he must work hard. So he resigns himself to the discomfort. He showers, has breakfast, and goes off to work. That night, he finds he sleeps longer and more heavily than usual.

So far, so, good. He goes out two days later to repeat the process. He has selected a three-day-a-week schedule, running one mile each time. He does his second run, returning bushed and sweating as before. He keeps up this pattern for all of about three weeks, by which time he misses his first exercise session — for a good reason, of course. It rains one day, so he postpones it until that afternoon. But that afternoon he finds it necessary to work late and has to put it off until tomorrow. Tomorrow he oversleeps and doesn't have time, but he says, "Oh, well, I only missed one day. I'll make it tomorrow for sure." The regularity of his self-punishment pattern begins to crumble, as he finds more and more things "getting in the way." A business trip, an overnight date, bad weather, oversleeping, and a variety of "reasons" enable him to exempt himself from his regimen, each time presumably for a special, just-this-one-time reason. By the time he has missed a full week or more of running, he simply lets the whole idea fade away.

Later, when he discusses the distasteful subject of getting into shape with friends or colleagues, he will probably say, "I hate to run. It's so boring. Maybe I'll try racquet ball or something. I need an exercise I can enjoy." So he may go the same route with racquet ball, tennis, or other forms of exercise. In each case, he overpunishes himself and drops it. He stopped running, not because it bored him, but because it made him physically uncomfortable. Even as his body began to adapt and get stronger, he poured it on too hard and found the entire experience distasteful. His misconceptions about the need to work hard and suffer during exercise — especially for males — prevent him from acknowledging the exertion as simply too much to tolerate, so he finds rationalizations to justify quitting.

He quit simply because his body, in its wisdom, rebelled against the punishment, and at an intuitive level he decided to give up on the program. Probably millions of people have tried repeatedly to get back into condition in this way, before discovering the necessity for nonpunishing exercise in order to make a habit of it. Many others haven't yet discovered this basic fact, and they continue to repeat the cycle of guilt, unrealistic exercise programs, overexertion, dropping out, and frustration, usually completing a cycle over a period of about one year.

If you'd like to make a sensible program out of getting back into good condition, you can apply the two policies of gradualism and nonpunishment in the following way:

1. Get a medical checkup and a clear go-ahead from your physician before you undertake this or any exercise project.

2. Give yourself a period of about six months to get back into fairly good shape, on the assumption that you will do a deliberately *limited* amount of exercise each week between now and then. Use the previously discussed AIDA model for selling yourself on a new habit.

3. Choose a good book on running from among the many available, read it carefully, and understand it thoroughly before you run.

4. Undertake a *heart-rated* running program, one in which you run slowly enough to keep your heart rate below a certain target level (as explained in the following section).

5. Buy a good pair of well-cushioned running shoes.

6. Never exercise at any time during this period so strenuously that you exert yourself beyond your comfort level, as established by your heart rate; don't let other people coax you or goad you into trying to keep up with them or compete with them; exercise in your own way, for your own body.

7. As you find your body beginning to change, and you begin to feel more energetic, stronger, and generally better overall, you'll appreciate the payoff; use your time-management techniques to *make time* for regular running; aside from an occasional slip, don't allow ordinary things to interfere with your objective of making it a rock-solid, regular habit.

8. As you slowly and steadily get into better and better condition, simply arrange your attitudes and your schedule to make it a permanent habit; instead of riding the roller coaster of getting into shape and then getting out of shape, maintain at least a maintenance level of regular running to keep you in good shape with a minimum of time invested; get into good shape and stay there.

9. Associate less with unhealthy, out-of-shape people, and more with people who keep themselves in good condition; read articles; discuss the topic with others, and in various ways keep it a high-priority item. As you get into good shape, you'll find yourself looking forward to exercise and not tolerating minor obstacles that might get in the way. Reinforce this attitude and this behavior in yourself at every turn.

10. By the end of the six-month period, you can easily and comfortably reach a level of conditioning, especially in your heart and lungs, as well as all the other organs, greater than that of about ninety percent of your fellow citizens. At that point, you can fairly easily shift your exercise project into a permanent part of your living pattern.

heart-rated exercise

The following recipe for finding your comfort zone and running within it can help you get back into shape without suffering. Again, get clearance from your physicain before proceeding with this or any other exercise project. These basic steps constitute a beginning approach:

1. Every time you run, wear a watch that measures seconds. Find out how your heart rate responds to exertion, which will give you a general idea of your true condition (not what you'd like to believe, based on your performance in high school or college ten or twenty years ago), in the following way:

a. While standing still, time your heart rate. Find your pulse on the inside of your wrist, or press your fingers into your neck just in front of the thick muscle that runs down on either side from your jaw to your collarbone. Count the heartbeats for ten seconds and multiply by six to get the rate in beats per minute. Many factors influence heart rate, but in general, the lower your static rate, the better your cardiovascular conditioning. A normal, out-of-shape person might have a standing rate of 85 or 90 beats or more.

b. Now walk very briskly for a period of one minute. Check your heart rate immediately. If it went above 120 beats per minute, your first half-dozen exercise sessions should consist only of brisk walking, about five minutes each time. Then move into very slow running, as described below.

c. If your heart rate stayed substantially below 120, then break into an *extremely* slow run, or a jog if you'd like to call it that, for another minute. Then check your heart rate. If it went above 140 beats per minute, you've finished exercising for your first session.

d. If it stayed between 120 and 140, which you can consider your *comfort zone for nonpunishing exercise,* run for another three minutes at the same slow speed to finish up your session for that day. Resist the temptation to run longer. It won't speed up the process.

2. If your conditioning level permits running rather than brisk walking, try a three-day-a-week schedule, either on alternating days or a three-day combination with week ends off. Just make sure that you have a day of rest between running days, to allow your body to build its conditioning level to meet the demands made on it.

3. At each session, run slowly and for measured time periods. Pay no attention to distance and ignore other runners whizzing by you. Run within your heart-rated comfort zone of about 120 to 140 beats per minute. Think of it as a matter of racking up "heart minutes" of exercise in your comfort zone, which will over time add up to improve your cardiovascular fitness as well as overall body fitness.

4. To keep within your comfort zone and to prevent getting out of breath, use the "talk test"; run so slowly that you could hold a conversation with another person running along beside you. You'll probably find that your speed is quite slow—probably much slower than you've ever run before.

5. For the first half-dozen sessions, limit your runs to ten minutes or less. Run for the number of minutes which keeps your final heart rate below about 140. If you consider yourself far out of condition, and especially if you've become substantially overweight, try progressing in one-minute jumps. Run one minute the first session, two minutes the second time, three the third time, and so on through sessions of four through nine, and, finally, ten minutes. By the time you get to running ten minutes at a time, you'll notice a significant improvement in your stamina and energy level. From there, you can use your judgment about progressing further.

6. Do some stretching exercises before *and* after you run, to keep the muscles all along the backs of your legs loose and flexible.

controlled, heart-rated exercise offers a gradual, non-punishing way to get into good shape and stay there

7. By the end of six months, you can easily achieve twenty-minute runs three times a week, which will put you at a level of conditioning far above the general population, and probably quite adequate to maintain a high level of wellness.

reducing your weight

The problem of losing weight probably frustrates more people than any other single life change they might want to make. But exactly the same policies of gradualism and nonpunishment apply to this as to the problem of getting back into good physical condition. Before we review a workable recipe for getting rid of fat from your body, let's examine a few psychological blocks which sometimes make losing weight more difficult than necessary.

One very subtle factor, in my opinion, revolves around the semiconscious connotations of the word *lose*. We usually refer to the process as "losing weight." Conceivably, the person who talks about losing weight might have an intuitive reaction of reluctance, even though he consciously wants to get rid of fat. The connotation of "losing," in the sense of failing at something, might trigger a slight feeling of caution. In addition, we speak of losing something of value, as a matter of inadvertently and unwillingly parting with it. Again, on an intuitive level, we might not want to rush into something like "losing" weight, especially when it relates to our precious physical bodies. I have no objective proof for this hypothesis, but it does seem to warrant a revision of our statements about changing body weight. I suggest you exclude "losing weight" from your vocabulary hereafter and instead refer to "reducing your weight."

Another speculation along these lines applies much more to men than to women. From early childhood, growing boys learn a simple nonverbal lesson — "big is best." With very few exceptions, the biggest and strongest boys come out on top in the primitive pecking order that develops in the playground and the schoolyard. In a sense, "might makes right." Most males grow up wishing, consciously or unconsciously, that they could somehow get bigger and stronger than everybody else, "and then *nobody* could push me around." I speculate that most males, as they grow out of their teenage years, welcome the increased body size that comes with increasing maturity and cherish whatever feelings of physical significance and potency they can muster. As a typical male grows into young adulthood, gets married, and settles into a sedentary life-style, he will probably gain a significant amount of body fat. At a semiconscious level, he may have mixed feelings about getting overweight. In one sense, he finds it aesthetically unattractive to have his stomach hanging over his belt buckle, but at the same time the increased body weight makes him feel bigger, more substantial, and more physically potent. Just by glancing around, you can find many examples of men, in the age range of thirty to fifty, in whom the macho swagger has turned into a waddle, but the same signals remain: "I want everybody to see me as big, powerful, and potent."

If this hypothesis makes sense, it means that many adult males have mixed feelings about reducing their weight. It may explain why many police officers get overweight rather quickly when they move into less active jobs such as riding in patrol cars. The "Wyatt Earp" syndrome, the gun, the badge, and the uniform, combine with twenty or thirty pounds of extra bulk to give them a greater sense of physical potency. Some military people may fall into this pattern as well.

Another blocking factor comes from childhood programming. Many fat people belong to the Clean Off Your Plate Club. They eat everything on their plates, no matter how it tastes and no matter how much of it they have. How about you? Do you belong to the COYP Club? Would you go into a restaurant, get served a plate of mediocre food, and eat every bit of it? If so, where did that habit come from? Can you picture your mother standing over you as a child saying, "Clean off your plate! Think about all the starving children in China who don't have any food. Now eat that!" Somehow if you ate all your mashed potatoes, some kid in China wouldn't starve.

If you eat in restaurants frequently, as many professional people do, and if you belong to the COYP Club, you'll probably steadily gain weight, because most restaurants serve about twenty percent more food than a typical adult needs at a typical meal. You can resign your membership in the COYP Club in two stages. First, for a period of at least a week, deliberately leave something on your plate, however small, at every single meal. Defy the childhood programming often enough and you'll soon set it aside forever. Recognize that the "waste" of the food took place when it came out of the kitchen, not when you left it on your plate. Second, begin to make a practice of stopping when you no longer feel hungry. Tune in to your body, sense your hunger signal, and "listen" for the moment when it shuts off. With just a little practice, you'll learn to sense it immediately. At that point, stop.

Take a few more bites, perhaps, and then leave the rest. These two behavior changes will enable you to cut your calorie intake significantly without going on any kind of "diet" at all.

To counteract some of these semiconscious blocking factors, any person, man or woman, can make a conscious redefinition of his or her basic body image as trim, athletic, powerful, and substantial without the presence of fat. He or she can then conceive of the fat as an unwanted extra mass, which will go away gradually under the influence of a moderate exercise program and relatively simple changes in eating habits. Unless staying fat solves some kind of a semiconscious problem or brings some unrecognized payoff, just about anyone can reduce his or her weight with a conscious approach.

If you'd like to reduce your body weight, you can apply the two principles of gradualism and nonpunishment by reducing your calorie intake just slightly below your body's maintenance level and letting the fat burn off slowly by natural metabolic processes. If you try to reduce your weight by a crash diet, what happens? Usually, the same kind of thing that happens when you undertake a crash program to get back into good condition. First, guilt about getting fat, then an unrealistic crash diet, self-punishment, giving up, and frustration. After a few weeks of dieting, you quit, and by about the same time next year, you begin the cycle all over again. But by reducing your weight *gradually* and without seriously distorting your eating habits, you can enjoy the process for the good feelings it brings, and you can make it permanent.

Let's review the mathematics of fat. First of all, *calories do count.* The calorie value of the food you eat corresponds directly to the quantity of fat your body stores, after it has used enough of the food to meet its energy needs. Think of a pound of blubber as equivalent to about 3,500 stored calories. Your body has a certain maintenance level, or a number of calories it needs on the average day, based on your age, gender, physical size, metabolism, and activity level. For example, if a thirty-year-old female needs 2,500 calories per day to maintain a constant weight level, and she eats 2,700 calories per day, in about eighteen days she will have gained a pound from the 200-calorie-per-day surplus. If she eats only 2,300 calories per day, she will have eliminated a pound of fat in about eighteen days. No amount of self-delusion, rationalization, or fad eating can obscure the basic mathematics of fat.

Incidentally, you can still get fat on a low carbohydrate diet. Carbohydrates supply only one of three sources of calories. Proteins and fats supply the other two. One gram of carbohydrate supplies about 4.1 calories of energy. One gram of protein also supplies about 4.1 calories . One gram of fat, however, supplies about 9.3 calories! You can see that you could easily take in more calories from fats in your diet than from carbohydrates. A "diet" of steak and salad could conceivably supply as many calories as a full fare, with various foods in balanced proportions.

Let's synthesize a recipe for reducing your body weight, based on gradualistic and nonpunishing behavior change. Try the following steps:

1. Use the AIDA model to really sell yourself on the benefits of reducing your weight; really want to do it.

2. If you belong to the Clean Off Your Plate Club, resign your membership.

3. Avoid all crash diets and fad eating programs; take a six-month view, at least.

4. Review your diet and get rid of the obvious junk foods and any concentrated sweets you can easily do without; balance it up and include a variety of healthy foods you like to eat. Don't eat "healthy" foods you don't like.

5. Don't bother to keep calorie consumption records, unless you want to do that for a week or two to get an idea of the approximate levels for various foods. Instead, just choose a few items to eliminate, in order to create a daily average deficit of about 100 to 200 calories — certainly no more than about 300 calories. At this level, you can eliminate a pound of fat every two weeks to a month, without any particular feeling of deprivation. You can easily do without a few hundred calories, and if you will have the patience to pursue it over a few months, you can reduce your weight easily and painlessly.

6. Try eating a light lunch, without liquor, and see how much better you feel the rest of the day.

7. Combine your weight-reduction project with a gradualistic and nonpunishing exercise project, as previously described. Over a period of weeks and months, the calories expended in running (or other exercise) do indeed accumulate to make a significant difference in eliminating stored fat. You will also feel better, increase

your overall motivation level, and increase your metabolism somewhat, causing you to eliminate stored fat faster.

8. Weigh yourself in the nude at the same time each day on a very accurate scale. Buy a balance-beam scale if you like; it will last for many years. Give yourself a mental pat on the back every time your weight stays down or drops further.

9. Get encouragement from other people. Make it a positive project and take your time.

how to stop smoking

Of the three most common atrocities against one's own wellness — getting out of shape, getting fat, and smoking — smoking probably gives more trouble than any of the others when it comes to changing habits. The vast majority of adult smokers realize, at least semiconsciously, that smoking steadily degrades their health, and they want to quit. Only teenagers, for whom, ironically, smoking symbolizes "being grown up," truly want to smoke. But, by the time they reach early adulthood and no longer have such simple illusions, most of them have become firmly hooked on nicotine stimulation.

Although most adult smokers want to quit, a large majority of them don't really believe they can. So, rather than face the prospect of trying and failing, which brings a painful reminder of the level of dependency they've developed, they just go along with it. They suppress the negative health evidence and develop convenient rationalizations to justify continuing. If we had a simple, painless, and convenient trick by which people could unhook themselves from cigarettes, the tobacco industry would probably collapse, virtually overnight. But we don't — so far — and advertisers for tobacco products realize that they merely have to supply encouragement and rationalizations for already hooked adult smokers and confirm the image among teenagers of smoking as something that sophisticated grown-ups do, and the sales just move along briskly.

If you currently smoke, and you've decided to take another try at getting unhooked, you can multiply your chances of succeeding manyfold by approaching it systematically. First, decide to stop altogether rather than cutting down. Don't torture yourself with a long, drawn-out, halfway effort, which has less chance of succeeding than getting rid of it altogether. It doesn't have to feel like a "cold turkey" operation if you prepare yourself for it effectively.

Try the following general approach:

1. First, use the AIDA model discussed previously to really sell yourself on getting tobacco out of your life. Stop blocking out the facts about health damage and go the other way; immerse yourself in information that persuades you and reminds you about the effects of smoking on your heart, blood vessels, bloodstream, liver, lung function, throat, vitamin balances, and so on. Your local office of Blue Cross, American Cancer Society, or American Lung Association will probably supply you with some interesting reading matter for this part of your project. *Don't underestimate this step;* really look into it, and you'll have very little trouble selling yourself.

2. Make a systematic inventory of "smoke signals" in your various environments, that is, the cues that trigger your mechanically programmed habit of reaching for a cigarette. Write down as many of them as you can identify and keep the list around where you'll see it.

3. Once you've sold yourself on your objective, pick a date no more than ten days hence on which you will stop completely. On that day, don't smoke the first one; throw away all your tobacco *and* your ashtrays, clean out your house or apartment, get rid of the smell, and freshen up the place. Clean out your car and deodorize it as well. Have your clothes cleaned to get rid of stale tobacco odor.

4. If possible, make a mutual-support agreement with your friend or mate; remind and encourage each other.

5. Declare your home a no-smoking area; don't permit guests or even your closest friends to smoke in your home. Do the same with your office or workspace.

6. Systematically eliminate as many smoke signals as you can from your environment — cigarettes, cigars, ashtrays, matches, lighters, cigarette advertisements, and whatever else you find.

7. Pay direct attention to cigarette advertisements as you read magazines; don't let them creep quietly into the edges of your consciousness; analyze them and recognize the suggestive, manipulative ploys they use to keep smokers hooked.

8. Sit in the nonsmoking section when riding on trains and airplanes and, if possible, when eating in restaurants.

9. Don't undermine your project by playing games with yourself like "just this one," or by trying to get someone else to take the responsibility for "catching" you and fining you or otherwise acting as a parent; *you* started smoking and *you* must stop.

10. Start a gradualistic and nonpunishing program of aerobic exercise at the same time you get rid of cigarettes; the increased activity of your cardiovascular system should speed up the process of cleaning out the chemical garbage from your bloodstream. You will also probably find your motivation much increased as you begin to get back into good condition.

11. Set a specific target period, say six months, without a cigarette, before you relax and stabilize your new habit. Don't preoccupy yourself with the project so much that you burn out and give up; take a long-term, patient approach.

12. From time to time after you've gotten rid of tobacco, reaffirm the sale and remind yourself how much better you feel; complement yourself for acting more responsibly in maintaining a high level of wellness.

SOCIAL COMPETENCE: GETTING ALONG WITH OTHERS

DEVELOPING
AN EFFECTIVE
INTERPERSONAL
STYLE

self-awareness

Each of us has a characteristic interpersonal "style," or habitual pattern of behavior in dealing with others. Some people talk very little, some talk a lot, and some talk a moderate amount. Some people seem habitually gloomy, grim, cranky, or irritable; others seem characteristically cheerful, friendly, and positive; and others vary between these extremes. We see shy people, obnoxious and aggressive people, and socially competent people who get along with others very effectively.

If we think of this category of social competence as a learnable set of skills, we can identify specific behaviors that work well and those that don't work so well in dealing with others. You can review your own habitual ways of behaving, and if you find some habits that seem to work against you, you can change them. In this way, you adapt to what you find out, and you become progressively more competent.

Self-awareness plays a very important part in our fourth competence category of social competence. To the extent that you pay attention to your behavior, pay attention to the actions and reactions of others toward you, and choose ways of behaving that get positive results, you transact with others adaptively and succesfully.

Consider a person you know who seems clumsy, crude, and inept in getting along with others. You can probably identify specific actions or habits he has that put other people off, make them angry, or cause them to shake their heads privately and make a mental note to minimize their dealings with him. You might refer to this person as a "bull in a china shop," a very descriptive metaphor. The bull in the china shop crashes into situations without sizing them up and without considering various subtle factors which can profoundly affect the situation. He pays too little attention to the reactions of other people, and he thinks very little about the impact his behavior has or might have on them. He has one or more major "blind spots" about his behavior. He needs to learn some basic things which most other people have already learned fairly well. His lack of learning works against him, and his extreme lack of self-awareness blocks his learning process.

Most of us have also seen another common behavioral syndrome, that of the "sandpaper personality." This person seems consistently and unwaveringly bent on putting other people down, off, or out. His hostile manner, either overt or covert, leaves others feeling like they've had sandpaper or a wire brush rasped across their tender skins. This abrasive interpersonal style might include frequent put-downs, cutting remarks, "playful" insults and criticisms, arguments, debates, accusations, and snubs. This toxic pattern originates in extreme incompetence at mood control, and an extremely deficient self-estimate.

The chronically abrasive person tries to empower himself, that is, feel potent and significant, by getting one-up on others. He usually has very little idea how intensely other people dislike his actions and how he undermines his own effectiveness with them. The abrasive interpersonal style and a managerial job usually form a deadly combination. These people tend to make the worst possible managers, because they habitually service their weak egos and deficient self-estimates at the expense of those whom they manage.

Although these two syndromes constitute fairly extreme behavioral patterns, probably all of us can profit to some extent by studying our own interpersonal behavior more closely, to see whether we have some toxic habits we might want to eliminate and whether we might want to adopt some useful habits. We can take the mystery out of this idea of self-awareness by developing an inventory of the most common types of problematical behavior and contrasting those actions with constructive and adaptive forms. Then, it becomes a relatively simple matter to assess our own actions in terms of their effectiveness in dealing with others.

attractive behavior
and repulsive behavior

Let's draw two contrasting profiles of interpersonal behavior, one of which tends to make it difficult for others to deal with us and one of which tends to make it easier for them. In the simplest sense, we tend to attract others to us by certain things we do, and we tend to repel them by other things we do. We can think of a person who habitually attracts others as having a predominantly *attractive* interpersonal style. The person who habitually puts others off qualifies for the label of a *repulsive* interpersonal style. We can also describe these two patterns as *toxic* and *nourishing*, respectively. We can array these two polarities along a continuum scale.

For example, talking too much and too loudly goes down on the repulsive side of the ledger. Sharing "air time" and modulating one's voice properly go down on the attractive side. We can inspect a variety of specific behaviors in this way. The examples of repulsive and attractive behaviors in Figure 10–1 should serve as a useful starting point for a personal inventory. The more you study the behavior of others and study your own behaviors with this repulsive-attractive model in mind, the more constructively self-aware you become, and the more effectively you can adapt your interpersonal behavior to get what you want while maintaining positive relationships with most people, most of the time.

fig. 10–1: repulsive behavior and attractive behavior

REPULSIVE BEHAVIOR INCLUDES:	ATTRACTIVE BEHAVIOR INCLUDES:
Withholding "strokes;" negative strokes.	Giving positive and unconditional strokes.
Throwing verbal barbs, "zingers."	Kidding positively.
Giving nonverbal put-downs.	Giving positive nonverbal strokes.
Discounting others' worth.	Affirming others as worthwhile persons.
Soliciting approval excessively.	Speaking and acting as an equal.
Losing one's temper easily.	Deferring one's automatic reactions.
Playing games with people.	Cooperating; giving positive strokes.
Disagreeing routinely; countering.	Agreeing where possible.
Confusing others, evading issues.	Levelling with others.
Violating confidences.	Keeping confidences.
Breaking promises and "contracts."	Making only those promises one will keep.
Flattering others insincerely.	Giving honest compliments.
Joking at inappropriate times.	Joking constructively.
Talking too loudly.	Modulating voice carefully.
Monopolizing a conversation; rambling.	Sharing air time; asking questions; listening.
Interrupting others frequently.	Hearing the other person out.
Changing the subject capriciously.	Staying with the subject; letting it evolve.
Speaking dogmatically, inflexibly.	Using semantic devices; conveying flexibility.
Complaining excessively.	Giving constructive suggestions and solutions.
Asking loaded or accusative questions.	Asking straightforward questions.

fig. 10-1: repulsive behavior and attractive behavior *(cont'd.)*

Overusing "should" language.	Offering suggestions and information.
Making offensive or crude remarks.	Respecting feelings of others; choosing words.
Insisting on having one's way.	Compromising; helping others.
Giving someone the "hard sell."	Suggesting; advising; negotiating.
Making demands of others; nagging.	Accepting others; negotiating.
Attacking or criticizing others.	Confronting constructively.
Inducing guilt in others.	Persuading honestly; stating one's wants.
Ridiculing others; embarrassing them.	Supporting others; laughing with them.
Shooting down others' ideas.	Suspending judgement; listening.
Patronizing or "parenting" others.	Speaking as an equal.
Giving unwanted advice.	Giving information and ideas.
Bragging; scoring "status points."	Sharing the other person's experiences.

toxic specialties

Some people develop toxic, repulsive interpersonal styles around just one or two well-practiced put-down strategies. They find these techniques so useful and effective in empowering themselves at the expense of others that they adopt them as permanent behavioral specialties. Because they lack sufficient self-awareness and perceptiveness about the reactions of others, they continue to undermine their own personal effectiveness by opting for ego-building instead of relationship-building. Three of these particular toxic specialties deserve special mention here. It behooves each of us to think carefully about our habits in dealing with others and to make sure we minimize or eliminate them.

First, we have the general purpose put-down, or what some people call "zingers." Apparently harmless when used rarely, the quick verbal slap, the barb, the cutting wisecrack, the slur on someone's capability or lovability, and the gratuitous insult all hurt. Whether a person subjected to these little one-up maneuvers shows it, he or she certainly doesn't appreciate it and reacts to it with withdrawal, caution, and a desire for revenge. After some years of studying human behavior, I've concluded that throwing zingers at other people even occasionally tends to undermine one's relationships with them to some extent, creating a slight edge of tension and wariness where a positive, relaxed interaction would work better.

The habitual zinger-specialist may say, "Oh, it's all in fun. Why make such a big deal out of it?" And when someone confronts him with the facts about his hostile interpersonal style, he may come across with another zinger: "Don't be so sensitive. Can't you take a little joking?" He usually uses these ploys to avoid facing the facts that his attacks irritate, annoy, and often hurt other people, and that he gets in the way of his own larger objectives in dealing with them. Two of these zinger-specialists doing battle provide an excellent example of subterranean hostility, with their forced laughter masking the dead seriousness of the ego-battle going on between them. I would advise anyone to eliminate the use of zingers from his or her behavior, to the greatest extent possible, and permanently. They serve no useful purpose in interpersonal dealings, and they can and do arouse needless hostility, resentment, and antagonism. By adopting the "no-bust" policy, that is, the deliberate habit of affirming people instead of "busting" them in your day-to-day dealings, you make yourself attractive, safe, and comfortable to spend time with.

A second way of "busting" people, the *discount*, goes further and works more cruelly than the ordinary zinger. In transactional analysis terms, to discount someone means to say or do something to him that attempts to make him feel small, insignificant, or less worthy than others. A discounting remark usually aims at the other person's feelings of inadequacy or insecurity, and it often has the purpose of hooking an automatic reaction of one-downness. By analogy, the discounter seems to say, figuratively, "I hereby mark you down in value from one dollar to seventy-nine cents. You don't have the same worth as other people."

Discounting remarks might include a slur against one's racial, national, or ethnic origin, an unkind remark about one's physical features, ridiculing one in front of others, poking fun at one's ineptness or lack of expertise in some pursuit, slurring one's masculinity or femininity, or labelling one in such a way as to indicate subordinate or inferior status. An action or a remark constitutes a discount if the user intends it as a put-down — consciously or as a matter of semiconscious habit — *and* if the recipient experiences it that way. For example, a man in an organization might refer to the women there as "girls," signalling consciously or unconsciously that he wants to deal with them as members of a subordinate and socially powerless group. Some women might experience the remark as extremely discounting, while others might not have a strong reaction to it.

Although unconscious discounting in various forms plays its part in undermining interpersonal rapport, the conscious and more direct forms of discounting seem to take their toll more severely. Monitor the things you say and do to others from time to time, and note the extent to which you acknowledge, accept, and affirm them as completely worthwhile human beings. Taking into account possible differences in formal authority, general social status, and qualifying credentials, do you still treat people who are waiters and waitresses, clerks, bank tellers, customers, teenagers, subordinate employees, and those in various service capacities as sovereign human beings, entitled to feel worthwhile and significant? Although the chronic discounter may have too much of an ego-stake in this strategy to acknowledge it and change it, most of us can eliminate this kind of toxic behavior by increasing our awareness of it.

The third toxic specialty worthy of particular study here, the *transactional game*, involves a more complex and subterranean form of one-up tactic. This particular syndrome probably merits your reading a book on transactional analysis, because it occurs so frequently in human interaction. Basically, a transactional game as defined by psychologist Eric Berne, who developed the theory, consists of an apparently innocent "offer" to play, usually a statement or action by one person inviting the other to respond in a certain way. For example, one love partner might insist on a display of affection from the other, such as an intense kiss, at a socially awkward or unacceptable time, such as in some public situation. "T.A." parlance refers to this as a child-to-child interaction. The other person, according to game theory, has a "gimmick" which the player can "hook," setting the other up for the attack that "scores" the point. In this example, the second party might decline to return the affectionate behavior, citing the inappropriate circumstances and possibly his or her own feelings of discomfort with the first person's demands. This unwillingness to display affection in such a situation constitutes the second person's gimmick.

Now, the first person scores the point by a role reversal, the characteristic phenomenon of a transactional game. He or she suddenly switches from the Child-to-Child level of affection to the Parent-to-Child level, with a scolding remark like "You never want to show any affection! You're so up-tight it's ridiculous!" Or the player might switch to the Child-to-Parent interaction with the pouting remark, "All right, *be* that way! You never show me any affection! You don't care about me at all!" In either case, the one-upped party ends up feeling ambushed, bewildered, and emotionally jarred. This disconcerting feeling constitutes the game player's "payoff." He or she has scored on the other party, often within the context of an ostensibly close romantic relationship, which has, nevertheless, a subterranean level on which a continuing power struggle proceeds. Other payoff emotions elicited by transactional games include anger, guilt, and jealousy.

All three of these toxic specialties serve exactly the same purpose for the user, in different ways. They have the effect of giving him feelings of personal power, by one-upping another person. They represent a squalid kind of a power-feeling, an illegitimate one. For the person with a relatively low level of self-esteem and a weak self-estimate, they provide the only source of power-feelings he knows.

As we grow and mature, and especially as we learn to empower ourselves and feel significant most of the time, we progressively discard these more primitive and self-defeating kinds of tactics. We adopt positive, affirmative patterns in dealing with people because we no longer need the others.

giving and getting "strokes"

In the parlance of transactional analysis, the useful term *stroke* means any message, verbal or nonverbal, that acknowledges another person's existence. Positive strokes include friendly greetings, honest compliments, affectionate touching, smiles, and so on. Negative strokes include angry statements, insults, accusations, put-downs, and the like. Some discounts, as discussed previously, have an even worse effect than simple negative strokes, since they may imply that a person doesn't or shouldn't exist. Some people unintentionally discount severely disabled people by not looking at them, or by avoiding even looking in their general direction. Looking at a disabled person just as you would look at anyone else, for just as long and with just the same level of relative interest and curiosity, constitutes for that person a positive stroke. It acknowledges his or her personhood.

Content-oriented strokes include those in which the recognition of the other person takes the form of a communicated message, such as a statement about something he has done which the stroke-giver chooses to praise. *Content-free* strokes include those in which the medium itself carries the message, so to speak. This would include "meaning-less" messages like "hi, there," "after you," and "thanks." A *name-stroke* serves as a very useful positive stroke, because almost all people react positively to hearing someone else use their name with a friendly tone of voice. Using content-free strokes often works well in affirming very shy people, or those with such weak self-estimates that they deflect or cancel out content-oriented strokes like compliments or honest praise. They experience the simple affirmation of hearing their name, for example, and can't easily say something that will neutralize the positiveness of the stroke.

People vary considerably in the extent to which they freely give strokes to others, and also in the extent to which they seek and accept strokes from others. Each person has a characteristic "stroke style," which he typically learned in early childhood and adolescence, and modified to a greater or lesser degree in growing to adulthood. People who, as children, received a goodly supply of positive strokes from the adults in their lives tend to give and get strokes rather freely as grown-ups. They will generally greet you spontaneously and in a friendly way; they will say pleasant things to you, and they will spice their transactions with you with honest compliments, positive kidding, and other kinds of positive strokes.

Those who got a steady diet of negative strokes in childhood tend to grow into adults who either give negative strokes to others, or who withhold strokes from others, giving them very stingily and more negatively than positively. Most people tend to copy the stroke styles they experienced in their formative years, making these patterns the primary means by which they give and get strokes — or avoid giving and getting them — all throughout their lives.

You can assess a particular person's general stroke style, in terms of quality and quantity, simply by watching him or her for a while. In a relatively short period, if you see this person in a variety of situations, you'll see the general trend of his or her interactions. You can also assess your own stroke style in the same way. You might want to review this extremely important aspect of your interpersonal style and judge the extent to which you think your overall pattern promotes positive reactions on the part of others you meet and deal with.

If you seldom say hello to people, rarely engage in small talk, keep your transactions to the minimum required to do business, seldom smile at others, rarely joke or laugh with them, and seldom compliment them, you have adopted a very frugal stroke style. You don't give much of yourself to them, possibly because you feel more powerful by cutting them off from you than in affirming them and helping them to feel good — and possibly because you think you wouldn't feel any better yourself by helping them feel better.

One can also go overboard in giving strokes to others and in trying to get them. The puppy-dog style of the "approval junkie" exemplifies the oversocial stroke style. If you figuratively hang around someone else's neck, stroking them at every opportunity, "shopping" for compliments and praise, greeting and stroking others effusively and insincerely, you might also undermine your effectiveness by leaving them feeling as if they had just taken a bath in warm molasses. The overly "theatrical" conversational style, with plenty of dramatic gestures and extreme voice modulation, fits into this category as well.

Probably more people tend toward the frugal than the oversocial stroke style. If you study your own style for a day or two, you can get a clearer idea of how it compares with others and how well you feel it works for you in most situations. If you want to increase your use of positive strokes with other people, you can do so in easy, graduated stages. Try greeting people regularly. Try nodding to strangers you pass on the street and exchanging greetings with those few who seem willing to do so. Say something in small talk to the person you see in the elevator every day. You can also form the habit of using name-strokes in talking with people you know, even — and especially — those you know well. Make it a policy to use the other person's name at least once during the conversation. If you think a person looks especially nice today, say so. If someone close to you does something nice, thank them especially well. Give praise and honest compliments to the people you work with, or who work on your staff if you manage.

Experiment with your stroke style from time to time. Make sure you use strokes reasonably freely with other people, within the range of "naturalness" you've defined for yourself as positive and constructive. Observe carefully how people respond to positive strokes, and you'll see what a powerful, effective, and constructive part stroking can play in your interpersonal effectiveness.

affirming others

The "no-bust" policy of dealing wih people pays ample dividends and plays an important part in helping you get what you need and want from other people while maintaining positive and enjoyable relationships with them. Describing this policy in positive behavioral terms, we can define it as a matter of habitually, consistently, and routinely *affirming* other people. If you make a habit of affirming people as you deal with them, you become absolutely magnetic to them. They want to deal with you again; they want to return for more, because most of them get such a steady diet of cold shoulder from the cross section of their fellow humans that they experience it as a downright treat to interact with you. Coupled with an attitude of high self-esteem and confidence, the affirmative behavior pattern will make more friends than you know what to do with.

In specific behavioral terms, affirming others means saying and doing things in the course of dealing with them that invite them to feel good about themselves for the most part. Although you can't always agree with another person, and the two of you may find your objectives in conflict you can, on the average, acknowledge him as a worthwhile person and show that you accept and respect him.

This translates, for example, into giving him a chance to express his ideas, listening attentively and respectfully to what he says, acknowledging his views and values whether or not you agree with them, cooperating and compromising when possible, emphasizing agreement and consensus when appropriate, proceeding from points of agreement rather than disagreement in discussing a matter, paying honest compliments, and finding and acknowledging the best in him. The affirmative style incorporates the various behaviors shown in Figure 10–1 on the Attractive side of the spectrum. It says to the other person "I consider you an important, worthwhile, sovereign human being, and I will treat you that way."

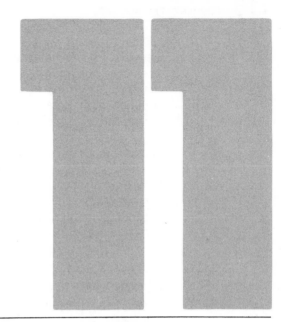

COMMUNICATING
ADAPTIVELY

So many people seem to pay little or no direct attention to communication as a process in itself, until it goes haywire. Then they talk knowingly about a "communication problem." In order to communicate effectively, you must consciously "read" the communication situation from time to time and adapt your behavior as necessary to accomplish whatever ends you have.

Probably the most significant skill in communicating adaptively lies in striking an effective balance of personalities, that is, in accounting for the other person's ego and controlling your own. By helping the other person and yourself to feel adequately empowered, you eliminate or avoid many of the most common clashes and misunderstandings, and you maintain a level of rapport which makes it easy to achieve your particular objectives in dealing with that person.

accounting for
the other person's ego

We all know that people bring their egos to every situation they meet, and that they act and react in terms of the relative degree of ego-sufficiency they feel. We know it, but most of us forget it too often. We can become so preoccupied with our own objectives, or our own egos, that we jostle the egos of others and inadvertently undermine our own effectiveness. By consciously accounting for the other person's ego, you can get along much more positively and effectively than by simply plowing ahead blindly.

Accounting for the other person's ego in a situation requires two conscious strategies: anticipating the most likely ego reactions the other person might have, based on your knowledge and experience, and eliminating from your behavioral repertoire those actions that tend to jeopardize the other person's ego and make him feel attacked.

You have attacked or undermined another person's ego whenever you treat him in such a way as to reduce his feelings of social adequacy or personal autonomy. A high-pressure salesperson, for example, reduces a potential buyer's sense of autonomy, that is, freedom of independent action, by aggressive or manipulative ploys such as refusing to hear "no," making remarks that make him feel guilty for not buying, or not giving him a chance to express his ideas. Very few high-pressure salespeople ever get a second chance to sell to the same customer. Hardly anybody wants to come back for more of the kind of treatment that makes him feel trapped, inadequate, or unsure of himself.

To what extent might you attack another person's ego, perhaps without fully realizing it? Or, to what extent do you deliberately attack another person's ego, building your own ego at the expense of his? In studying your own interpersonal behavior, you can easily identify and eliminate the obvious blunders like the one-ups and put-downs listed in the earlier section under Repulsive behavior. You might also pay attention to more subtle forms of ego attack, such as "topping" someone else's achievement or good fortune with "That's nothing. Wait'll you hear this." Do you usually top another person's joke with "a better one"? To what extent do you shoot down ideas before other people even get them out of their mouths? Do you tend to preach to others, or lecture them about what they "should" do and how they should act? Do you overuse "why" questions, by pointedly questioning the motives of others? Do you tend to squelch the opinions of others, with flat statements like "You're wrong" or "You don't know what you're talking about"?

Accounting for the other person's ego in a constructive way means no "busts," no one-ups, no put-downs, and an affirmative, cooperative pattern of behavior in dealing with him.

controlling your own ego

A folk ballad attributed to John Pryne asserts that "Everybody's got to have somebody to look down on, who they can feel better than at any time they please." Probably more human misery, animosity, misunderstanding, antagonism, and even warfare comes from the inability of human beings to maintain a sense of personal power and their tendency to try to steal it by clobbering other human beings, than from any other cause.

Controlling your own ego, together with the strategies just described for accounting for the other person's ego, gives you the flexibility and adaptability you need in getting along effectively in your affairs. In addition to abandoning put-down behavior, make sure you also set aside the more subtle forms of ego-building which often make others feel less attracted to you. Some of the more subtle forms of ego-building in which many people indulge include:

1. Bragging.
2. Name dropping, place dropping.
3. Scoring "status points" by talking about one's expensive car, house, neighborhood, clothes, jewelry, and such.
4. Overusing "me-talk", that is, dwelling on self-description and self-assertion at the expense of the other person's interests.
5. Continually trying to "outsmart" others by coming up with *the* solution

to a problem, *the* way of doing something, or *the* explanation for something; pretending to know everything about everything.

Instead of weaving a bragging remark or report into your conversation, with a superior tone of voice, try sharing it with the other person. You can say something like "I've got some good news to share with you. I just got promoted," or whatever it may be.

By learning to empower yourself, using the psychomotor skills of mood control described in Chapter 6, you can do without ego-building tactics and add a whole new dimension of versatility to your dealings with others. By continually feeling powerful within yourself, respecting and affirming yourself, and holding yourself in high regard, you don't need to try to feel superior to others. You already have the ego-sufficiency you need to function effectively in dealing with them.

avoiding deadlock

How many times have you watched two people embroiled in a self-reinforcing ego-battle, with the facts and issues of the situation thrown out the window? How often have you seen a simple difference of opinions escalate into a "personal" matter, with all glands involved and secreting maximally? How often have you gotten into one of these donnybrooks yourself, and later regretted it?

This counterproductive, win-lose deadlock situation merits recognition as a major human relations syndrome. First, two people doing some kind of business bump into a point of disagreement. Without thinking, one of them will attack the other's ego instead of the problem. He may do this in an overt, obvious way, with a statement like "You're an idiot! You obviously don't know what you're talking about!" Or he might do it in a more subtle but just as disturbing a way, such as raising his voice a bit and adopting that characteristic pitch and intonation pattern that says nonverbally, "You're an idiot! You obviously don't know what you're talking about!"

The second person responds to this ego-attack by marshalling facts, quasifacts, figures, accusations, rationalizations, distortions, and whatever else he can muster for a counterattack aimed at the first person's ego. After a few exchanges, they enter a mutual downward spiral into a give-no-quarter-and-ask-none, win-lose deadlock. By the time they get their egos fully invested, significant cooperation becomes virtually hopeless. They fight it out, undermining their own individual objectives, and destroying the basis for their continued relationship in the future.

Some protagonists may even institutionalize their deadlock, carrying it on and nursing it for years. If they manage separate departments in a business organization, they may infect their respective staff members with their antagonism, making working-level cooperation much more difficult. If they would simply stop and think about the larger perspective of their interaction, they could see the damaging effect of the deadlock and act adaptively to eliminate it.

You can deal with deadlock best by preventing it from ever occurring. You can adopt the personal policy exemplified by a popular bumper sticker often seen in California: "Thou shalt take part in no bad scenes." Some years ago, I made an unusual personal decision and a very conscious one. I decided to stop arguing with people. Simply that — stop arguing with them, stop countering them, stop blocking their egos. I found the change in the quality of my life quite amazing. Of course, I didn't stop working to achieve my purposes in the various situations I met. I merely stopped arguing and found better ways to change people's minds.

If you pay careful attention to the egos involved in a situation, yours and the other person's, you can usually prevent deadlock, foster a cooperative attitude on his part, and leave yourself maneuvering room to solve the problem or achieve your objectives in alternative ways. Keep these simple policies in mind in dealing with others, especially when deadlock seems to threaten:

1. Don't attack the other person's ego; it will only backfire on you.

2. Don't box the other person in; leave him room to change his behavior, change his mind, or compromise without any loss of face.

3. Offer options for him to choose from; don't try to limit him to only one avenue of your choosing; respect his autonomy.

4. Compromise whenever possible; make it a win-win situation by building in benefits for both of you.

You can still aim for and achieve most of your objectives in dealing with others, while accounting constructively for their egos and preventing deadlock. Just don't confuse your ego with your objectives.

listening as an interpresonal strategy

You can talk and you can listen, but you can't very well do both at the same time. While you operate your mouth, your brain can't take in and process much of the useful information that constantly flows all around you. In the simplest sense, you have but two communicating modes: transmit and receive. To deal with other people effectively, you need to balance these two modes consciously and expertly. Sometimes you profit by moving information from you to others. At other times, you serve your purposes best by getting the information flowing to you. Knowing when to do which forms the basis of the skill of listening.

Let's think of listening as much more a matter of perception than politeness. Although the usual viewpoint about listening as a matter of affirming the other person and showing interest in him does indeed make sense, careful listening plays a much more important part in your transactions with others; it enables you to *find out things you need to know.*

Those who don't listen effectively as a routine matter in day-to-day dealings with others, either because they talk too much, talk at the wrong times, or simply preoccupy themselves with things that distract them from the subtle aspects of the situation at hand, usually undermine their own effectiveness. They destroy rapport with others and prompt others to assess them as ineffective and unreliable at exchanging ideas and information. They tend to confuse themselves with fragments of information, half-understood ideas, distorted explanations of complicated situations, and superficial accounts of subtle matters. They also tend to confuse others as they pass on the fuzzy and distorted gleanings from their inefficient conversations. They often embarrass themselves by acting on the basis of their misconceptions and distorted viewpoints; they contract "hoof-and-mouth" disease in conversational situations. Because they don't listen consciously, extensively, and effectively, they stay relatively ignorant, uninformed, and unenlightened.

How would you assess your own listening capability? To what extent do you maintain an investigative attitude, scanning, searching and enquiring about what goes on around you? Do you generally share "air time" on a fairly equal basis? For example, when having lunch with two other people, do you generally talk less than one-third of the time? Do you usually let another person finish his sentences? Can you listen attentively, without jumping the gun, second-guessing, or countering the other person, while he finishes describing an idea in its entirety?

If you like to talk, and especially if you usually do have many useful things to contribute, you might want to experiment with the amount of talking you do. You might choose to settle for saying less in various situations, in order to keep your eyes and ears open and find out more. You don't have to have something to say about every topic that comes up. Get on the receiving end as often as possible. You often learn when you listen.

Study the possibilities for using questions effectively. You might want to simply increase the number of questions you ask of other people in various situations, about various matters. You never know when an innocent question might lead to a very valuable piece of information you didn't know existed. Think of the questions you can ask as divided into two categories, *divergent questions* and *convergent questions*. Divergent questions invite the other person to answer broadly, with a variety of information, and dealing with various points of view. They often begin with phrases like "What do you think about . . . ", "What do you suggest we do about . . .", and "In what ways can we . . .". Go easy on convergent questions, which invite much narrower, more specific answers. These include questions that solicit only certain specific facts or figures, questions that invite the other person to answer in terms of a few stated alternatives, and yes-or-no questions.

Yes-or-no questions, sometimes called *binary* questions, often tend to narrow the discussion unnecessarily, especially when used extensively. When you ask a person a yes-or-no question, you've given him a prescription for the answer, and you may have unknowingly blocked off some useful information he has and could share with you if you invited him to do so. Make it a point also to steer away from *leading questions* and *loaded questions*. The leading question tries to put words into the other person's mouth and, more often than not, encodes the questioner's own opinions or values. A question that begins with "Don't you think that . . ." really amounts to an opinion with a question mark at the end. A loaded question tries to manipulate the other person into a self-damaging response, and it usually causes trouble between the questioner and the respondent.

By paying close and continuing attention to the direction of the flow of information in your dealing with others, you can choose when to transmit and when to receive. You keep valuable information coming your way, and you learn and adapt effectively while achieving your objectives most of the time.

explaining ideas clearly

You've probably noticed how widely people seem to vary in the ability to explain something clearly, simply, and effectively. One person gropes around for words, gets tangled up in complicated details, and bounces back and forth from one fragmentary idea to another, trying to get them to hang together somehow. Another person organizes what he has to say effectively and explains an idea clearly, with a minimum of fumbling and a minimum of wasted words. In a society like ours, the command of the written and spoken word plays an extremely important part in getting ahead. Those who have developed their verbal skills extensively seem to influence others more readily and get what they want more often than those who haven't. Some recent evidence suggests that verbal skills have steadily declined in America, especially among younger people, possibly because of the amounts of time they spend in the passive, nonverbal experience of watching television. Whatever the reason, you don't have to look far or listen for long to hear someone who seems only marginally articulate and able to deal with only the most commonplace and concrete verbal concepts.

How do you feel about your own verbal fluency? How would you rate your ability to organize a concept and get it across to someone else? Perhaps you'd like to develop this particular competency, and you'd like to have a systematic way of approaching it. Let's inspect the most common descriptive malfunctions in human conversation and identify some specific strategies for organizing your words and getting them under control.

Most people who fumble with their words get tangled up in only a few basic malfunctions, such as:

1. Not getting the other person on the same wavelength; launching off on a question, description, or explanation without choosing a convenient starting point which the other person can readily understand and appreciate.

2. Getting into details too soon; jumping directly into nitty-gritty specifics without giving the other person some kind of a big picture to fill in as they go along.

3. Insufficient generalizing; telling too much, giving much more detailed information than necessary, and including tangential or irrelevant information.

4. Rambling; giving needed information in random order, without choosing a sequence or a logical starting point; hopping from one item to another, sometimes without completely explaining one before going to another, in such a way that the listener can't anticipate and organize what comes next.

We can subdivide the skill of verbal fluency into two main components: having and using a large and versatile *vocabulary*, and using various *descriptive strategies* to lend structure and order to what you say. With respect to your vocabulary, the total number of words you know and *use* determines your verbal capability. Knowing a word doesn't count for much if you don't make use of it. Many people feel reluctant to speak fluently and to draw upon the more subtle or sophisticated terms in their vocabulary, perhaps out of a lack of confidence about using them correctly, or for fear of sounding pretentious. If you feel unsure about your vocabulary, you can get any number of useful vocabulary-building books at a general bookstore. Take one of the diagnostic vocabulary tests you can find in them, and get an idea of the size of your recognition vocabulary. If you feel it needs expanding, get to work on it. You might find it one of the most useful investments of time and energy you can make.

If you already have a large and versatile vocabulary, and you make a habit of deploying it effectively, then you need only develop your skills at using the various descriptive strategies that follow:

1. *Matching wavelengths* — get the other person squarely on your wavelength and ready to comprehend what you have to say; use a *focus statement* that tells him what you plan to talk about and where you propose to begin, for example, "I'd like to discuss the financial portion of the project plan with you, and specifically the cash-flow projection, so we can finish writing up the plan and publish it." Don't just walk into his office and hit him cold turkey with something like "How did you estimate the materials costs for Project X?" He probably has many other things on his mind, and he needs a few seconds to swing his attention fully around to the matter you want to discuss.

2. *"Scoping" the conversation* — choose a level of detail, specificity, or concreteness appropriate to the objectives of the conversation; avoid the "watchmaker" syndrome, that is, if he wants to know the time of day, don't start telling him how to make a watch. Make it a conscious choice whether to scale your description at a high level of generality or a very detailed and complete accounting; choose the big picture, the nitty-gritty details, or somewhere in between, but choose consciously.

3. *Organizing and sequencing* — choose a particular logical framework for organizing what you have to say; then proceed to hang all the individual bits and pieces on it, one at a time. You can use any of several ways of organizing the things you say, such as:
a. *General-to-specific* — start with a summary statement that gives the other person the big picture; then proceed to go into more detail if appropriate. Train yourself to make a one-sentence summary of an idea or a situation, so you can do it easily when the situation calls for it.
b. *Specific-to-general* — give a well-chosen fact, figure, or specific feature to establish a starting point; then proceed to enlarge and fill in the rest of the picture.
c. *Subdividing* — start by identifying the logical "pieces" of the subject; mention each of them to give an overall perspective; then proceed to describe them further one by one, if appropriate.
d. *Sequencing* — go through the natural sequence of the events or processes you want to describe; link them all together to give the other person a sense of logical time-flow.
e. *Logical chain* — describe the sequence of cause-and-effect relations

involved in some result; use a series of "if-then" statements or "there-fores" in order to give the other person a sense of logical continuity to your explanation.

4. *Telegraphing* — before you go into the details of your explanation, and after you have matched wavelengths and scoped the conversation, tell the other person which of the above organizing strategies you plan to use. For example, you might say, "I'll describe for you the sequence of steps in the process by which a company gets unionized. First, . . . etc." In this way, the other person knows ahead of time where you plan to go with the discussion; he can anticipate some of the things he will hear, and he can set up a system of "pigeonholes" in his mind, filling them in with the items of information as you give them to him in logical order.

5. *Semantic flexibility* — use very few so-called allness terms, such as all, every, everybody, nobody, and never; replace these with terms that describe degrees of things and that delimit your statements and make them realistic and nondogmatic. Avoid flat, categorical statements, especially critical value judgements, and use semantic qualifiers like "in my opinion" "to a certain extent," and "so far as I know."

You can use these same general strategies in asking questions of others. Tell the other person how you would like to have the answer organized, if the situation makes this practical. You might say, "I don't really understand the procedure for handling X. Would you tell me which departments get involved and then give me a quick summary of what each one does?" Don't just blurt out a half-organized question and expect to get a well-organized, easily understandable result.

Teach yourself to pay more attention to the descriptive processes you use in dealing with others. Deploy your vocabulary effectively, pay attention to communication "maintenance" processes like matching wavelengths, and develop your skills at using the various organizing strategies. Learn to edit what you have to say, eliminating irrelevant bits and pieces and staying carefully on the main road. Consciously choose a logical approach to use in explaining your ideas, and you'll maximize that portion of your social competence which depends on influencing other people with words.

changing someone else's behavior

I can't change your behavior. Only *you* can change your behavior. Similarly, you can't change someone else's behavior; only that person can change it. You or I or anyone else will only change our behavior for a good reason—"good" from our own point of view, not necessarily from anyone else's. Keep this in mind in trying to get another person to behave differently.

Many people needlessly burn a great deal of energy in trying to force others to do things or stop doing things, without accounting for the real motivations of those they want to influence. If you ever hope to influence another person, you must find, establish, create, or communicate to him *a reason* to behave differently. Few people would argue outright against this seemingly self-evident principle, yet many people persist in trying to impose demands on others or make requests of them that offer no benefits *to them*.

Many parents, for example, try to change their children's behavior by scolding, nagging, or browbeating. A father may contintually fight with his teenaged son or daughter about smoking, without realizing that smoking provides perceived benefits for the youngster and giving it up would not. Giving it up might bring the alternative benefit of getting dad off the youngster's back, but then he'd probably just find something else to nag about. So, for the teenager, continuing to smoke makes sense. Dad fights a losing battle because he refuses to accept the reality of human motivation — that people have their own "good" reasons for behaving as they do — and *his* reasons why they should behave differently simply don't matter.

From the foregoing reasoning process, we can extract a kind of formula, or general approach, to inducing someone to change his behavior in some way. You can go through something like the following steps:

1. Get a clear idea of what you want the other person to do or to stop doing. Make it specific and realistic; don't waste time trying to get people to do things that they don't find valuable.

2. Find or create the necessary benefit for the other person — the reason that will enable him to find doing what you want more attractive than what he currently does. This may involve a subtle or abstract benefit, such as good will or a sense of satisfaction in helping someone, as well as some more tangible benefit.

3. Consider simply asking him to do what you want; start with the direct approach before you turn to more roundabout strategies, especially for relatively small matters. If you account for his ego, use a positive approach, and ask for what you want tactfully and matter-of-factly, you will probably have a very good chance of getting it.

4. If you've decided that the direct approach probably won't work, make a plan for influencing his behavior by changing your own. Think of the other person as placed within an overall situation, to which he reponds; your behavior constitutes one of the "inputs" to the situation. You may not have consciously thought about it, but

the other person does indeed respond to what you say and do, in conjunction with the other stimuli he gets.

5. Define a consistent behavioral pattern for yourself in dealing with the other person, so that your actions will reinforce certain things you want him to do and not reinforce the behavior you don't want, in the classical Skinnerian sense of operant conditioning. For example, you might deal with the negative-stroke person by breaking eye contact whenever he gives out a negative stroke, by turning your attention elsewhere for a few seconds, or even by standing up as if to leave, or actually leaving the room. When he says or does something positive, you can give him your attention more closely, smile, and lean forward to reinforce your nonverbal rapport with him. By having a clear idea what you want him to do, and a definite procedure for reinforcing it, you can more or less "shape" his behavior by shaping yours.

COMMUNICATING ASSERTIVELY

Probably about one person in four has at least a moderate degree of difficulty in getting what he wants and having his own rights and interests tended to in dealing with others, because of a lack of assertiveness. The current high level of interest in assertiveness and assertive communication techniques testifies to the importance and usefulness of this particular skill area. In addition to having and using the skills of communicating adaptively as described in the previous chapter, the effective individual needs the skills of communicating assertively, in order to achieve a balance of personalities and interests in the situations in which he finds himself.

Specialists in assertive communication training usually contrast two extreme styles in dealing ineffectively with other people, identifying them as *passive*, or underassertive, and *aggressive*, or overassertive. These two polarities, as illustrated by the continuum scale of Figure 12–1, correspond to the two behavioral styles we investigated in Chapter 5, the capitulator and the compensator. The capitulator has trouble speaking up, requiring others to deal with him fairly, defining his basic human rights, and taking the initiative in dealing with others. The compensator, or aggressive person, has trouble in accounting for the egos of others, and compromising and cooperating with them; he thinks he has to win over them whenever possible, rather than come out even.

The central region of the continuum scale of Figure 12–1, which we identify as the *appropriately assertive* style, constitutes a pattern of dealing with others which accounts for your needs and their needs at the same time. In this chapter, we explore some specific techniques for doing that.

knowing what you want

So many underassertive people get psychologically swindled, intimidated, manipulated, and talked out of what they want in situations, because they go into them with no clear idea of their rights, privileges, and entitlements. An underassertive employee may go into the boss's office in hopes of getting better job assignments and having certain inequities corrected. But when the boss questions him, especially in a certain tone of voice, he may lose his nerve, retreat, fumble over his words, and finally settle for what little change the boss considers worth making.

Probably he couldn't say, in so many words, what he wanted. And the boss couldn't read his mind. This person could multiply his effectiveness manyfold in improving his situation by adopting

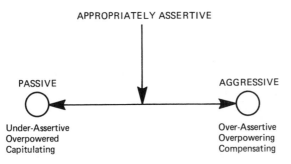

APPROPRIATELY ASSERTIVE

PASSIVE

AGGRESSIVE

Under-Assertive
Overpowered
Capitulating

Over-Assertive
Overpowering
Compensating

fig. 12-1: an adaptive, appropriately assertive style achieves a balance between your interests and the other person's interests

one basic strategy: *deciding clearly what he wants* before he gets entangled with other people in trying to get it. In this example, if the employee had sat down privately for a while, made a list of possible changes the boss could make, selected a few as high-priority items worth shooting for, and worked out a persuasive sales pitch to show the boss how things would get better, he could probably have come away with much more than he did. You can think on your feet much better if you don't have to think on your feet. Preparing for a situation enables you to adapt to what happens much more effectively than going into it cold turkey.

In deciding what you want out of a situation, you must estimate what you and the other people involved will consider "reasonable." This means setting aside your own self-doubts and feelings of inferiority and defining, in specific, operational terms, a fair deal. If you feel guilty and apologetic about returning some item to a store and asking for your money back, and yet you don't consider it unreasonable when someone else does it, you've probably set a double standard for yourself. Deep inside, you don't grant yourself the same rights as you grant to the rest of the people in the world.

In considering such an action as asking the bank officer to cancel what you consider an unfair service charge against your account, for example, ask yourself this question: If I worked at the bank and a customer came to me with this request, would I consider it reasonable? If you answer "yes," then go and do it. Separate your own feelings and apprehensions from the situation, settle on what a reasonable and prudent person would consider a fair and realistic expectation, and then take action to get it. Other people will find it very difficult to try to dissuade you by their little intimidating and manipulative tricks when you ask for something that, deep down, they themselves consider reasonable. And, if you ask for something definite and you stick to your guns, they can't very well side-track you from your objective.

thinking on your feet

Let's use the idea of thinking on your feet as a foundation concept for communicating assertively, and let's give it a more specific definition. We can consider thinking on your feet in a situation as coming up with something to say or do which helps you get the results you want. This leads us immediately to several important and related notions.

First, as previously mentioned, it means you must have a good idea of what results you want out of the situation. Decide what you consider fair and reasonable, and adopt that as a goal in going into the situation. The difference between having a specific goal in a situation, and simply wandering into it with only a vague notion of what you want, may spell the difference between coming away with a useful outcome and coming away feeling frustrated and defeated.

Second, our definition of thinking on your feet implies having a *preestablished repertoire* of things you can say or do that tend to get the reactions you want from others. This includes, for example, the adaptive strategies described in Chapter 11. It also includes certain specific *verbal tactics* you can employ to influence other people while protecting your self-esteem. If you have a great deal of trouble in this particular area, that is, in feeling defensive, intimidated, guilty, or unsure of your rights, it might pay you to read a complete book on assertive communication, from the many good ones available in general bookstores.

Useful verbal tactics for operating under pressure include:

1. *Broken record* — make a brief statement which explains to the other person, simply and unequivocally, what you want. Keep saying exactly the same thing over and over, declining to get sidetracked by manipulative ploys, until you get what you want.

2. *Fogging* — instead of defending yourself against criticism from another person, just acknowledge the critical remark and proceed with the problem-solving process. For example, you could say, "I agree with you. I should have kept the receipt, but unfortunately I've lost it. But, since the item still has your store's sales tag on it, I'd like to have my money back." Or, you might say, "You may have a point about my arriving late. The problem we have to solve at this point, however, is XYZ."

3. *Bargaining* — once you've gotten the other person to accept you as somebody he will have to deal with, and you've politely and confidently asserted your basic rights in the situation, offer him a workable compromise. Propose a settlement or a course of action that will take his ego off the hook and that will get you most of what you want.

130

Dealing with criticism warrants special attention here. Most of us have learned three standard reactions which we tend to use when someone starts criticizing. Typically, a person will tend either to *deny*, *defend*, or *counterattack*. He may debate with the other person about whether he did a certain thing, or whether he deserves the blame for something, citing evidence to prove his point. Or, he may try to defend himself from getting the blame, by citing reasons why he couldn't help doing what he did, or why he couldn't control the situation for which the other person wants to blame him. And third, he may try to fight fire with fire using the "well, so did you" ploy, accusing the attacker of committing some act as bad as or worse than his own alleged misdeed.

None of these techniques works nearly as well, over the long run, as the technique of fogging does. When you fog in the face of criticism, you figuratively become a fog bank, refusing to put up the resistance the other person expects. Most people have learned to criticize others, and then to overcome their defenses and denials, but they get completely disoriented when the other person fogs in the face of their attack. They've worked out an attack for every defense except "no defense." By granting the point of their criticism, which often deals with something in the past that doesn't have a primary effect on the issue now at hand, you disarm them and zero in on getting what you want. Whether you consider the criticism "true" makes no difference. You have no obligation to deny, defend, or counterattack. You can simply acknowledge the criticism and go right on.

Having used one or more of these techniques in a pressure situation, you can think on your feet effectively by "keeping your eye on the ball." This means keeping in your mind a clear idea of your goal for the situation — the result you want to come out with. If you know what you want, and you use some of the verbal tactics just described, you can make sure other people don't sidetrack you with issues and ploys unrelated to your goal. This means not getting hooked into feeling defensive or angry when someone attacks your ego, not letting them make you feel guilty, and not getting distracted by every little "red herring" they drag across the trail to divert your attention from the main issue.

You can also maintain effective mood control in such a situation by *centering* yourself, that is, taking a few seconds to relax a bit, boost your personal power feelings, and develop a sense of relaxed, adaptive readiness to deal with the situation. Also, make up your mind that the world won't come to an end if you don't get what you want out of the situation. Don't make it a do-or-die expedition. Just make a reasonable try, and if the other person or people involved don't see it your way, accept that fact and adapt to it. You might also try to solve the problem in two sessions, getting them warmed up at first, then returning later to offer a bargain or to complete the process. Accounting for the egos of the other people also makes sense in this respect. If you don't box anyone in, and you offer them a face-saving way to cooperate or compromise, you often get what you want while helping them get what they want.

"owning" your feelings and reactions

All of us learn, as we grow up, certain implied social rules about emotions and about allowing others to know about our emotions. We learn that, in certain situations, we can let others see the way we feel without getting into trouble. We also learn to conceal our feelings in certain other situations, and even to more or less overcome our feelings in certain situations and go ahead with whatever we feel we have to do. The key to reasonable emotional freedom lies in knowing which situations call for which approaches, and in not locking ourselves into rigid patterns.

Some people have trouble modulating their emotions, and consequently they tend to have trouble staying on an even keel much of the time. They need to develop the mood control skills described in Chapter 6. Others, by contrast, have more or less over-learned the process of self-control, to the extent that they become emotionally flat, unexpressive, unresponsive, and constrained to behavior patterns that don't involve the risk of getting emotionally aroused in any way. They define for themselves an emotional comfort zone that channels them too narrowly. In effect, the emotionally overcontrolled person fears his own emotions, so he avoids situations that threaten to arouse them.

Such a person may have grown up among people who punished him, either physically or psychologically, for any display of emotion, positive or negative, and he learned not to provoke them. Some adults who have this extreme emotional overcontrol deny that they ever feel hostile or hurt or apprehensive or anxious or even happy. Not only can't some people cry or get mad or get hurt, they also can't laugh. The grim, overcontrolled person often displays little sense of humor, or often at most a sardonic, cynical one.

Most of us agree that suppressing and over-controlling emotions works against our psychological health and well-being. Recent evidence also supports the long-held notion that suppressing strong emotion can have fairly direct physical consequences for one's body. Although it probably makes good sense to learn to modulate one's emotions and to learn to react within reasonable bounds, it also makes sense to understand and acknowledge whatever emotional processes one actually does have.

If you'd like to review this aspect of your functioning, start by asking yourself whether you tend to consider certain emotional reactions in yourself as basically "bad" and not worthy of a "good" person. Many people, for example, have to convince themselves that they never feel angry, because they concluded early in their lives that only bad people get angry. So, they have to lie to themselves in order to avoid having to label themselves "bad."

How do you tend to appraise your sexuality and your sexual reactions? Do you tend to feel a bit guilty about having a sexual impulse toward an attractive person of the opposite sex?

For men in particular: do you tend to feel a bit insecure about having a tender, nurturing impulse toward a baby or a young child? Do you tend to feel guilty and "unmasculine" about getting a tear in your eye when you watch an especially touching movie or play, or when you hear a certain kind of music? Do you tend to feel out of place and unmasculine about singing, dancing, or doing something artistically expressive? Can you laugh at yourself, gently and constructively?

By "owning" your feelings and reactions, that is, acknowledging them and accepting them, and furthermore asserting your right to feel however you feel in a situation, you tend to come into focus with the earthy, natural, "creature" side of your functioning, and you avoid working against yourself and your needs. If you own your feelings as a natural and precious part of your functioning, you won't allow others to take them away from you, and you won't have to try to pretend they don't exist.

recognizing your "grabbers"

Do certain things tend to get your goat easily? Can someone else say a certain thing, use a certain term, or speak to you in a certain way and reliably get a rise out of you? These "grabbers'" — things other people can say or do to trigger your negative emotions — can put you out of your emotional comfort zone if you allow them to. When you snap-react to something someone says or does, you suddenly lose mood control, and your cerebral cortex capitulates to your hypothalamus.

As you've grown up and matured through the years, you've probably learned to take more and more things "in stride." We use this metaphorical term to mean that you allow the potential provocation to pass on by, and you don't allow it to upset you. The more you can take things in stride and maintain positive mood control, the more you have matured. Perhaps you still have some grabbers which you haven't yet eliminated. You can maintain more effective mood control, keep your stress level within your comfort zone, and achieve your objectives more consistently if you can minimize the number of grabbers to which you respond.

Take a pen and paper and make a list of your most prominent grabbers. Keep the list handy and add to it from time to time. Think about *trigger words* to which you might react angrily or defensively, such as stupid, clumsy, fat, girl, boy, kid, or any slur against your ethnic, national, or racial origins. Identify specific kinds of inconsiderate behavior by others to which you react especially strongly. What minor atrocities can other people commit to put you in a bad mood? Study these grabbers and your reactions to them, and increase your awareness of your *signal-reaction* processes. Make up your mind that you will not let arbitrary signals from your environment disable your mood control. By becoming more aware of your remaining grabbers, you can steadily weaken them and finally eliminate them altogether.

overcoming manipulation

Sometimes the world seems to have two distinct subpopulations — the manipulators and the manipulated. Actually, each of us probably can shift from one role to the other from time to time, but it does seem that many people spend more time in one category than the other, and some people seem to manipulate or get manipulated a large fraction of their time. If you make a habit of manipulating other people — and you realize it — you probably need to think about the matter of self-esteem and investigate various adaptive communication techniques, such as described in Chapter 11, for getting what you want by straightforward means that don't leave other people feeling vaguely swindled.

If you feel that you fall prey to manipulation too often, perhaps you need to review some of your reaction patterns. Manipulation depends on a subterranean level of communication. When a person attempts to manipulate you, he wants something from you that he believes you wouldn't give him if he asked for it outright or offered to bargain for it. Also, he tries to conceal his direct interest in the outcome by focusing your attention on some ostensible benefit or "antibenefit" of interest to you. By antibenefit, I mean a condition which you don't want, that is, one you would find undesirable.

The benefit offered may consist of an apparent outcome which you presumably would find desirable, but which disguises an outcome the manipulator would find desirable for himself. By learning to ask one simple question — How will *you* profit if I act in this way? — either silently or directly to the person, you elevate the matter to the level of a consciously recognized sales pitch, and you can deal with it effectively there. If you'd like the other person to help you make up your mind, you can say so. If not, you can decline his persuasive influence and decide for yourself what you want.

The antibenefit approach centers around an emotionally undesirable consequence for you, usually one of the three primary emotional weapons of the manipulator, guilt, jealousy, or fear. By developing and maintaining a high level of self-esteem, you can eliminate these automatic reactions and zero in on the real issues of the situation. By returning to your own definition of your goals in the situation, by getting a clear idea of what you want and can fairly and realistically insist on, and by keeping your "crap detector" tuned in for the manipulative messages aimed at hooking your one-down feelings, you can force the manipulator to operate at the explicit level, rather than the implicit level of suggestion, innuendo, and implied obligations. Most chronic manipulators become as helpless as fish out of water when stripped of the protection afforded by the unspoken level at which the process goes on. When you bring the matter to the conscious, explicit level, you can communicate adaptively, assertively, and fairly.

handling criticism and compliments

Some people have as much difficulty dealing with compliments as dealing with criticism. Although we tend to think of the two as fundamentally different kinds of treatment by others, they relate very closely in terms of our reaction processes and our self-esteem.

People who get disabled easily by criticism usually also feel uncomfortable when praised or complimented. This happens because they have learned, early in their lives, to make their power-feelings at least partially dependent on what other people think and say about them. They have granted the evaluations of others — positive *and* negative — primary status in determining how they feel about themselves.

By reviewing the matter of self-esteem and your self-estimate from time to time, especially with respect to the notions of lovability and capability, and identifying the kinds of things others can say or do which make you feel less significant, you can begin to eliminate their effects. You can learn to place your self-esteem and your feelings of personal power more and more beyond the reach of the signals others send you.

You can use the technique of fogging, described previously, to deal effectively with the criticizer. Just make up your mind that no critical remark, no matter how relevant, how "true," or how sudden, should undermine your sense of worth as a person.

You can apply the same attitude in dealing with compliments by others. Instead of "deflecting" a compliment, that is, responding to it with a statement that disagrees with it, minimizes it, or otherwise weakens it, and thereby confirming an unworthy self-estimate, you can form the habit of simply accepting the compliment and saying "Thank you." Forbid yourself to make a countering or contradictory reply. If you really want to develop this skill, learn to say, "Thank you. I agree."

constructive confrontation

No matter how well you've learned to get along with people, and no matter how highly you've developed the affirmative skills of behaving attractively and accounting for the other person's ego, there will come times when you need to assert yourself forcefully and directly to get what you consider fair play in a situation. You may find your objectives in conflict with someone else's, or you may feel that the other person hasn't accounted for your legitimate needs and interests, and doesn't plan to. You need the communication skills necessary to confront the person directly and to try to influence him by controlled "force of personality." You can adopt a policy of *constructive confrontation* by combining the previously discussed techniques of adaptive communication and assertive communication with a simple strategy for approaching the other person directly and negotiating for a behavior change on his part.

Constructive confrontation need not involve animosity, adversary orientations, or even discomfort for either of the two parties, especially if both of them have a history of dealing with each other positively and adaptively. Let's consider the term *confrontation* to mean simply a direct approach to the other person, without the connotation of doing battle. From this point of view, you can use a constructive confrontation technique with a friend, colleague, mate or romantic partner, boss, employee, or anybody else you deal with.

The technique of constructive confrontation simply involves using some version of the following three steps and statements:

1. I don't like . . . — the behavior or situation you want him to change.
2. I want . . . — a specific condition you want and consider reasonable.
3. I'm willing to . . . — an offer to cooperate and compromise with him in bringing about the situation you wanted.

If you say these things politely, tactfully, adaptively, and assertively, you stand an excellent chance of getting a constructive behavior change while maintaining positive feelings all around.

13

MANAGING PERSONAL RELATIONSHIPS

realistic and unrealistic views
of relationships

Countless people have frustrated themselves needlessly in the matter of "relationships." Love relationships, parent-child relationships, relationships with friends, parents, bosses, coworkers, organizations, and institutions — all these offer opportunities for a person to make himself unhappy by adopting an unrealistic view of what he can get from others.

Many highly immature people rely too heavily on the concept of a "relationship" in trying to get their needs met, especially emotional needs or those related to self-esteem and the attention or affection of others. Such a person may talk about his relationship with his friend having gone sour, or his relationship with his parents giving him trouble. Many people talk about their relationships with husbands, wives, boy friends, or girl friends as needing repair.

A person may make unrealistic demands on another person, or try to manipulate the other person into doing something, in the name of some vague notion of the relationship between them. Many people use the term *relationship* freely in conversation, with only the vaguest notion of what they mean in specific, behavioral terms. They may argue with others, browbeat them, nag them, or try to make them feel guilty, invoking the idea of the relationship as the basis for their demands.

Probably, the use of the term *relationship* as an abstract noun causes more of the trouble than any other single factor. Many people speak of a relationship as if to describe some concrete, tangible thing, which they could somehow see and touch. They describe it as lasting a long time, getting stronger or weaker, growing, fading, or dying. This metaphorical habit of description tends to distract their attention from the matter of their own behavior, and it tends to preoccupy them with vague, abstract, and elusive "qualities" of the so-called relationship as if it existed as a separate entity, external to themselves or the other person.

For immature people especially, this concept provides a ready-made way to transfer responsibility for the results in their lives to an outside agency — the relationship — or to another person. This view assumes that the other person's part in the relationship somehow places certain automatic, inescapable, and "natural" obligations upon him to behave in certain ways. It may also mean for the immature person, although often to a lesser extent, accepting certain obligations placed upon his own behavior by the supposed relationship.

You can steer around many interpersonal tangles and misunderstandings with respect to the idea of relationships by adopting the more realistic view based on *two individuals* behaving toward one another in ways calculated to get their respective needs met or to accomplish their respective purposes. It makes more sense to study the people and their behavior, rather than the "relationship" between them. If you want the other person to behave differently, you'll have to change your behavior to get the result you want. Nagging, pouting, and making demands in the name of "our relationship" will have little effect if the other person doesn't see a value in changing. Similarly, demands by another person that you change don't make sense if the change doesn't involve good reasons for you, from the point of view of your needs, feelings, and values. Let's use the term *relationship* sparingly, and keep an eye on its connotations when we do.

the concept
of personal responsibility

You can make a great deal of sense out of your long-term interactions with other people by thinking through the matter of *personal responsibility*. Returning to the definition of the executive attitude in Chapter 3, as involving the concepts of authority, responsibility, and choice, we can reflect on the matter of responsiblity from the point of view of obligations which people consider to exist among themselves.

Ask yourself these three general questions:

1. What responsiblities do I have for the lives of *other people*, the consequences in their lives, and their levels of happiness?
2. What responsiblities do other people have *to me* for the consequences in my life and for my happiness?
3. What responsibilities do I have *to myself* for the consequences in my life and for my happiness?

I hope you answered these three questions with "None, none, and 100 percent," respectively. Too many people imprison themselves by an unrealistic sense of responsiblity for the well-being of others, or by an unrealistic insistence that other people accept responsiblity for making them happy, or even both. When you understand that only you have the responsiblity for your life and happiness, you can free yourself from situations, behavior patterns, "relationships," and obligations that work against your values and lead you to feel unhappy or unactualizing.

Rejecting responsiblity for someone else's happiness doesn't mean that you don't care about it. It simply means that you expect *him* to take the executive role in bringing it about, and that you feel free to decide what part you will offer to play in his life, if any. The choice to feel happy or unhappy rests with him, and the problem-solving processes, decisions, and actions necessary to lead a happy life also rest with him. If you have a well-developed sense of responsiblity for your life, you can get along positively with the other person over the long run, without allowing him to substitute his needs and values for yours, and without trying to substitute your needs and values for his.

The archaic child in each of us doesn't like responsiblity; we've all learned to feel bad when we "fail." If we can get somebody else to take the responsibility, then we can revert to our six-year-old mode of expecting, demanding, and pleading that the other person make everything all right. If he fails to do so, we can just go on whining, expecting, demanding, and pleading; we don't have to change. We don't have to adjust our behavior and deal with the circumstances differently.

For people who tend to form strong, dependent attachments to others, either in the form of love relationships, hero-worship relationships, or emotional-support relationships, this idea of personal responsiblity comes very hard. They have probably lived most of their lives with the convenience of considering others accountable for their emotional well-being, however unsuccessfully, and it takes a considerable effort, with considerable self-insight, to move toward more self-liberating patterns of behavior.

Conversely, people who have lived their lives allowing others to expect, demand, and plead that they do whatever others feel their role/obligations entail, tend to feel very uncomfortable in saying "no" to unrealistic demands. They've become especially susceptible to guilt-induction, which highly dependent people have usually learned to use quite skillfully. Putting other people back on their own responsiblity takes steady practice for these people.

You might want to review some of your long-term relationships with various people and institutions in your life with respect to the concept of self-responsibility. See whether you want to make any changes in the ways you deal with them.

toxic relationships
and nourishing relationships

In reviewing the relationships you have with the various people who populate your life, you might find it helpful to make a general assessment of the relative benefits you get from having them in your personal orbit. Do some of them treat you in relatively toxic ways, as defined in our model of "attractive" and "repulsive" behaviors in Chapter 10? Do others affirm you as a person and treat you well for the most part?

Try constructing a toxic-nourishing "ledger" of your various relationships. Take a pen and paper and make two vertical columns. Label one "Toxic Relationships" and the other "Nourishing Relationships." Now begin to write down the names of various people you live with or deal with frequently, and with whom you have some personal choice-making possibilities about interacting. For those who seem to cause you more trouble than joy, write their names on the toxic side of the ledger. Put the names of those whom you instantly associate with good feelings and personal attraction on the nourishing side. Some names may give you mixed feelings; some positive aspects mixed with some negative aspects. Put these on the dividing line between the two columns if you like.

Then sit back and reflect on your assessment. If you have somebody's name on the toxic side, how do you plan to deal with that person? Will you simply continue to drift along with the situation as it is, or will you take constructive action to change it? For those on the border line, do you have a way to reorient your dealings with them so as to move them into the nourishing column? And for those you placed squarely in the nourishing column, to what extent do you consciously nourish and develop your positive "vibes" with them and let them know you appreciate the way they treat you?

In particular, you might decide to get some of the names off the ledger altogether. You might want to take direct action to eliminate the toxic influences of some people by getting them out of your life.

"firing" somebody from your life

Do you realize that, as the chief executive in your own life, you have the right to "fire" anybody from your life who doesn't play a positive role? Just as you could discharge an employee who refused to fulfill his acknowledged work responsiblities, so too can you give a toxic person his walking papers.

Getting rid of a toxic person, otherwise known as "breaking off a relationship," presents great difficulty for many people. Guilt feelings, apprehension over the possibility of conflict and hard feelings, and a sense of personal obligation toward the other person for some specific reason may all loom up to confuse and cloud your thinking when the time comes to take action.

You can develop a certain amount of skill at "firing" people simply by doing it the first time. Once you see that you can indeed tell someone in no uncertain terms that he no longer has a place in your life, and you overcome the potential guilt feelings, you'll see that the world hasn't come to an end and that your life and the other person's life both go on.

This may seem like a rather cold-blooded view, or perhaps an oversimplified one, but if you think about the matter in these terms, you may well find the idea of firing someone a useful and practical metaphor. If you've recently struggled with the idea of divorce, for example, you'll probably find that, after you sweep aside all the rationalizations you give yourself and take the matter of guilt and apprehension out of the equation, it reduces to a matter of actualizing your own values. You need to fire someone from your life when they consistently act to prevent you from actualizing certain primary values you have.

Some people fire whole organizations from their lives. A professional person might find the atmosphere and organizational values highly toxic where he or she works, and may make a direct decision to find another place to work with values congruent to his or her own.

In all cases, firing somebody from your life merely means taking direct action to construct and maintain relationships that align with your own needs and values.

MANAGING
LOVE
RELATIONSHIPS

Can you manage a love relationship? What a ridiculous question! After all, we know that people can't help falling in love, that "being in love" means "being totally committed," and that people in love can't help saying and doing the most irrational, irresponsible things. No one can analyze love, no one can understand it, and, in fact, no one can even define it. So how can a management consultant, of all people, presume to apply logical thinking techniques to this particular area of human functioning?

I suppose that about fifty percent of readers will part company with me at this point, having adopted and relied on certain fixed beliefs about romantic love all their lives. Probably what comes next will severely tax the credibility of many of them. If you put yourself in the category of people who firmly believe that we should declare the subject of romantic interaction between human beings beyond the range of systematic thought and immune to logical scrutiny — to say nothing of "management" — then please turn to Chapter 15 and continue reading.

On the other hand, if you believe that mature, effective, self-responsible, self-actualizing people can indeed cooperatively manage their romantic relationships, I invite you to read further.

realistic and unrealistic views about love relationships

Immature people tend to have highly unrealistic views of "love" and tend to use the term to rationalize and justify various dependent feelings, which don't seem nearly so noble when explicitly stated as they would like to think. For those with a low self-estimate and correspondingly low self-esteem, "falling in love" solves certain problems and exempts them, in their own minds at least, from responsibility for their own feelings and behavior.

Probably more people have confused themselves, frustrated themselves, and made their lives miserable by fuzzy and unrealistic concepts of "love" than for any other reason. Some people have killed themselves over love, or more particularly the loss or lack of it. Some have killed other people because of it, including the people they supposedly "loved."

Actually, those who make themselves unhappy and ineffective over love usually do so because they have fallen into a semantic trap. They have adopted unworkable behavioral strategies because they harbor fuzzy concepts which they have assembled from two very fuzzy terms: *love* and *relationship*. Many highly "romantic" people make a habit of saying "You can't define love." Actually, if they would

144

take that statement seriously, they could free themselves from a number of irrationalities. If, rather than flinging the abstract term *love* about, they would direct their attention to more concrete aspects of their functioning, specifically their behavior, they could think much more effectively about the business of getting their needs met for human contact and affection.

Semanticists give the name *objectification* to the process of talking about an abstract concept as if it had concrete form, as if one could perceive it with the senses, react to it as a physical entity, and deal with it in physical terms. We frequently objectify many of our abstract concepts and refer to them in terms of physical metaphors which help us think about them. But objectification becomes a perceptual-cognitive trap when we overrely on concrete metaphors which don't adequately describe our experiences in a framework that will help us solve problems and decide how to behave.

To objectify the abstract concept of love means to speak of it as a physically sensible entity. Someone might say, "My love is pure," using the notion of an unpolluted substance. Another might say, "Our love will bloom and grow forever." Does this refer to a tree? A flower? A vegetable? One might say, "My love is stronger than yours" or "Love will conquer all." This tendency to speak of love as a substance, an item of plant life, or a physical force can easily lead the person using these objectifying metaphors into a conceptual forest, leaving him unable to apply them to the day-to-day reality of dealing with another person in the matter of affection.

Many people also objectify the term *relationship*, describing it as strong, weak, growing, dying, or falling apart. Again, the use of these metaphors might help the speaker to organize his or her thoughts effectively, but they can also confuse him or her about the operational realities of interpersonal behavior. This happens particularly when a person thinks in terms of "making sacrifices for the sake of the relationship."

Other semantic traps people can fall into when trying to think about or describe affectionate relationships include the True Love trap, declaring that "This time I'm *really* in love; all the other times I just thought so"; the Selfless trap, based on the self-defrauding statement, "I care more about him or her than I care about myself"; and the Total Commitment trap, exemplified by the words of the song, "When somebody loves you, it's no good unless she loves you *all the way.*"

Let's use the term *love relationship* as simply a convenient general-purpose term, referring to an affectionate relationship between a man and a woman, with sexual activity involved or potentially involved. Rather than try to wrestle with the abstract connotations of the term, let's go to a more specific, operational level — the level of behavior. We can understand and manage love relationships better by thinking about the two people as separate individuals and by describing their wants and their behavior. The concepts discussed in this chapter apply equally well to marriage relationships and single relationships.

You can understand your relationship with someone of the opposite gender, you can assess it, and you can decide what to do about it, by asking yourself a few basic questions:

1. What do I want that he or she can supply?
2. To what extent does he or she now satisfy those wants?
3. What does he or she want that I can supply?
4. To what extent do I now satisfy those wants?
5. What additional values and wants do we have as separate individuals that we can't get satisfied by each other?

Question number five usually draws the dividing line, and it often presents a challenge to the reality-adaptation skills of one or both of the people who have a love relationship. To some people, the notion that the love partner would ever want or need anything they can't supply amounts to blasphemy, or at the very least a cruel or unkind thing to say or think.

Yet, probably each of us has been on both ends of an unbalanced relationship at one time or another, that is, having needs and wants which the other person didn't see fit to satisfy, and also not seeing fit to satisfy certain needs and wants which the other person communicated. Indeed, it makes more sense to conceive of an affectionate relationship as a means for satisfying many specific needs and wants for both parties, but not all of them. Realistic expectations of each other in such a relationship can go a long way toward ensuring that both parties get most of their needs met most of the time, while remaining free to pursue the other needs without unrealistic obligations.

The immature person typically seeks a dependent or mutually dependent love relationship, in which the other person becomes obligated to meet his needs for attention, affection, and approval, virtually all of the time. This unrealistic expectation of the other person leads the immature person to employ various subterranean "power" tactics to try to control the other one's behavior. These typically include manipulation, guilt induction, use of jealousy, nagging, and demanding. The immature person usually suffers from a continual sense of apprehension about breaking up. He or she senses, in some vague way, that his or her demands and interpersonal tactics tend to reduce the other person's autonomy, and that the other person might not stand for it indefinitely. However, he or she allows the childish desire for complete and permanent need-satisfiaction to block his or her perception of the discomforting reality.

For this reason, many love relationships settle into well-developed power struggles, with most of the action going on at the subterranean level, especially between two highly dependent and immature people.

The mature individual, on the other hand, considers a satisfying love relationship very important to his or her life, but not all-encompassing and not all-superseding. He or she thinks in terms of establishing positive relationships with various people of the opposite gender, with each person offering some advantages and some disadvantages in terms of his or her need-satisfaction and the other person's needs and values.

The mature individual refuses to give any abstract "relationship" full authority over his or her executive choices, and insists on viewing a love relationship as only one of a variety of needs and values he or she chooses to serve. When the other person no longer offers sufficient need-satisfactions in exchange for an acceptable range of expectations, the mature person feels free to explore possibilities with someone else who does. The immature person, on the other hand, often gets tangled in the hopeless, unrealistic, and confusing battle of trying to "save the relationship," clinging to the other person at the expense of his or her own self-actualization.

Managing a love relationship effectively requires the same skills as managing any other relationship, in terms of communicating adaptively and assertively. In addition, it requires some extra skills in the way of negotiating with the other person and getting a conscious agreement about how each person can get his or her needs and values accounted for. The techniques of *negotiating* and *contracting*, described in a later section, play an important part in this adaptive process.

The mature view of a love relationship leads to adaptive, cooperative communication between two people, based on low-tension give-and-take agreements, minimal use of ulterior forms of persuasion or influence, and maximum need-satisfaction and values-confirmation of both people.

All of the concepts discussed in this section apply equally well to married love relationships as to single love relationships.

the single state
and the married state

Love is an ideal thing; marriage is real. Confusing the real with the ideal never goes unpunished.

GOETHE

In case you hadn't noticed, singleness has in recent years attained the status of a respectable alternative to marriage. Although most Americans still seem to view marriage as an important aspect of life, and for some of them an essential part, more and more people choose single status without apologizing for it. Some also have it thrust upon them. This means that many people now have more options in arranging their lives, and in relating to members of the opposite sex, than they had, say, in the early 1970s, and certainly in the 1960s and earlier.

Singleness has grown rather quietly into a full-scale social phenomenon, just since the 1960s. We now see advertisements for "Adult Single Apartments," as well as apartments limited to singles only, families with children excluded. We have a single people's tax-rights movement. The divorce rate, that is, the ratio of divorces per year to marriages per year, has risen to well over forty percent nationally and approaches eighty percent in California. "Living together," formerly labeled "lewd and lascivious cohabitation," now generally has the status of another way to arrange one's life. It went from scandalous to just about commonplace in the space of one decade.

Company personnel officers now wrestle with employee benefit plans that provide for "spouse" participation, not knowing how to classify the employee's living partner. Many of them have settled for the descriptive category "spouse or equivalent."

The recent popularity of the single state — and particularly the tide of magazines, books, and movies that paint a fantasy picture of singleness as a life of constant excitement, filled with glamorous, romantic people, and nothing but exciting experiences — has caused some people more than a little consternation about their own lives and experiences. Many recently divorced people, for example, find that they have grossly overestimated the glamor of single life, and they have not adequately prepared themselves psychologically for the transition.

Many just-divorced people will jump determinedly into the social swim, going to every party they can find, cruising the mixer lounges, buying their disco clothes, taking dance lessons, and so on, in search of the "single life." After they exhaust themselves psychologically, physically, and financially, they may stop and review the situation, sadder and wiser, and possibly more aware of what they don't want as well as what they do want. They get a clearer idea of the kinds of people they enjoy spending time with, what they enjoy doing, and what compromises they will make in forming romantic relationships. For many just-divorced people, this adjustment becomes at one and the same time the most painful and the most rewarding of their lives.

Divorced women in particular often face severe adjustment challenges, especially women above the age of about twenty-five to thirty. Although many young women now coming out of high school can clearly see the various options for education, career, marriage, or a mixture, women who grew up before the 1970s generally experienced a socialization process that valued immediate marriage and a life-long role as mother and homemaker. Many a woman of age thirty finds herself in an unsatisfying marriage, either divorces her husband or gets divorced, and finds herself thrown into the job market with little in the way of saleable skills. If she followed the typical pattern prescribed by parents, peers, school curriculum, and cultural programming, she found a husband by the time she graduated from high school. If not, she might have had to go to college for a year or two, or perhaps work for a few years, until she could find a husband and settle down to making a home. Seldom did her environment encourage her to educate herself in a serious way, to acquire abstract mental skills, or to seriously consider a professional career. So, for her, education had little or no operational value.

Now, however, she finds herself in a situation where somebody has changed all the rules. The marriage they told her would last "til death us do part" just crashed, leaving her without a means of economic support, and the new rules of the game say that an able-bodied adult woman should support herself, and possibly raise one or more children with financial assistance from her ex-husband. She faces the prospect of starting at the bottom of the job ladder at age thirty or thereabouts and having to acquire marketable skills at the same time that she earns a meager living. Small wonder that many women in this cir-cumstance feel resentful and angry at the faceless "system" that put them into this situation. And small wonder, too, that many of them marry again "on the rebound," rather than go through the painful process of readjust-ing their lives.

This particular syndrome has spawned one of the fastest-growing areas of the industrial training market, namely train-ing programs for women dealing with management, communication skills, upward mobility, and career planning. With the divorce rate still rising, and more and more women opting for single status for longer periods of time, women have begun to insist on gaining fair and equal access to the job opportunities that men have always enjoyed.

For many professional people today, women just as much as men, the option of "single or married" presents some difficult challenges, in terms of organizing their lives, adopting the execu-tive attitude toward the choices involved, and forming love relationships that enable them to actualize most of their primary values most of the time. In a way, the old situation presented fewer difficulties only because it presented fewer options. Formerly, very few couples had to deal with the "two career" situation, because so few women had career oppor-tunities on a par with their husbands or living partners. Now, as more and more women catch up on career knowledge, skills, and experience, more of them find themselves choosing between a male partner and a career. Some find effective compromise arrangements; some cannot.

This has led, in part, to a somewhat stoical view of love relationships, which some people consider highly evolved and others consider tragic. Many professional people today, including women, find themselves in the position of more or less rationally weighing the pros and cons of a particular affectionate relationship and comparing it in the broader sense with other options, which include career or life changes.

One person might argue that this trend leads people to steer away from the more romantic, "committed" relationships, opting instead for superficial arrangements which they can give up when other values conflict. Others might argue that people now have more freedom to actualize their values in a variety of key result areas in their lives, and that the old idea of a head-over-heels dependent relationship, which outranked all other values, never did make sense from the standpoint of personal growth and self-expression. This area remains open to debate.

In any case, like it or not, we as professional people find ourselves confronted by choices and options unlike those we've known in the past. No longer does life hand us a standard script, based on a male part and a female part, separately defined as husband-provider and wife-homemaker. We find it necessary, in thinking over our wants and our values, to consider a variety of areas now — the various key result areas identified in Chapter 7 — and to work for an overall balance of rewards that maximize quality of life as we define it and that actualize most of our primary values most of the time.

divorce
and other "catastrophes"

Divorce means various things to various people. To some, it means the end of happiness, the *Gone With the Wind* of life. To others, it means the beginning of life, a time of liberation from past mistakes, and freedom to chart a new course. For most people, it means uncertainty, anxiety, and a tremendous demand for adjustment. Many things happen, and happen fast. The subject merits a matter-of-fact discussion here, because it affects the lives of so many epople, especially today.

Probably most married people dread the idea of divorce more than almost any other personal event short of loss of life or a major health breakdown. For many women in particular, the idea of having marriage end in divorce represents a personal failure of the first magnitude. The powerful social programming given to males as well as females in our society predisposes them to look upon marriage as a permanent, irreversible step, an irrevocable personal obligation, and the basic defining life-role expected of a normal adult. For some people who take the step, and eventually find that marriage to one particular person not only does not fulfill their lives, but indeed stands directly in the way of the actualization of their primary values, the idea of breaking up and starting life in a new way presents a powerful personal conflict.

For some, it entails guilt — profound, unshakable, irrational guilt about denying one's life-role and about putting the other person on his or her own. For others, it spells failure in this important role, and perhaps inability to attract and hold a mate. Most people who go through a divorce have a great deal of difficulty with it because of the deeply embedded social values they've learned.

Deciding whether or not to divorce one's partner involves a fundamental appraisal of one's needs and values, and a reassessment of the possibilities for actualizing them through some version of the present relationship. If you have a decision to make in this regard, you can reduce some of the anxiety and simplify the thinking process somewhat by approaching it fairly logically. First, you need to clarify your primary values, as discussed in Chapter 7. Try writing down a list of important wants you have, such as career, social activities, education, travel, material things, affection, sex, time alone, and so on. The more comprehensively you think about these, the more effectively you can assess the situation.

After identifying the disparity between what you want and what your present situation gives you, you next have to ask: Can I realistically expect to change the situation, or get the other person to change his or her behavior, in such a way that I get enough of what I want to warrant continuing to live with this person? If you answer "yes," then you probably have a problem in communicating adaptively between the two of you. By rebuilding your communication channels, and by negotiating and contracting as described in a following section, you can probably reorganize the situation to make the relationship much more nourishing than toxic.

However, if you answered "no" to the question, you know what you must do if you want to get started living effectively again. The problem then shifts to one of getting up the nerve and energy to make the break, and adapting to the temporary upheaval it will probably involve.

For many people, however, the answer to the question comes up "I don't know." Quite often, "I don't know" really means "Probably not, but I can't face the trauma of breaking up, so I'll avoid the issue and continue to drift with the problem." Drifting with the problem, however, probably represents the least effective of your options. If you feel this way, you might want to return to Chapter 7 and review the idea of the Santa Claus fantasy, that is, the tendency to "wait for Santa Claus" or somebody to come along and set you free from your circumstances. You got yourself into it, and you must get yourself out of it.

In this case, you can return to the question and restate it in this way: If I could somehow snap my fingers and become completely free of this person and this situation — divorced — with no strings attached, no pain, no strain, and no unpleasant side effects, would I do it? If you answer "hell, yes!" you have separated the problem into its two basic components, deciding to do it and actually doing it.

If you have decided to get a divorce, or if your mate has informed you that he or she wants a divorce and will not entertain alternatives having to do with continuation of the marriage, your problem becomes one of adaptation to reality, constructive action, and maintaining an even emotional keel through the process, which probably won't turn out as horrible as you expect. Over one million people get divorced each year; you can do it too.

To put the divorce process in perspective, think ahead about a year or so and make a fairly specific definition of the kind of life-style and activity pattern you would like to have at that point. Consider that your aiming point, and deal with the divorce process as just a territory through which you must navigate to get there. Remind yourself that the way you look at it makes all the difference. If you adopt a positive attitude about your goal, and if you practice the various mood control and communication skills previously discussed, you will probably find that you can communicate at least fairly maturely and adaptively with your future ex-mate, and make the experience a reasonably dignified and constructive one for both of you.

growing together and growing apart

We live now in a time of disparate values. Alternative life-styles, alternative ways for men and women to relate to one another, new ways of defining the basic roles of male and female, careers and professions for women, new ways of raising children, of communicating values to them — all these have given us more choices in our lives. But with choice comes ambiguity, uncertainty, and sometimes anxiety. Sometimes in making our choices, we can't find an option that satisfies all of our wants, or actualizes all of our values. We must compromise, and for some people compromising comes harder than simply accepting whatever option life thrusts upon them.

The idea of "breaking up," and especially

breaking up a marriage, brings different reactions to different people. To some, it means failure and personal tragedy, while to others it means adaptation and readiness for continued growth and development of one's life. I suspect that the solid, reliable man-woman relationships of the good old days when mom and dad grew up and got married lacked a few valuable assets that some of our modern options offer.

Certainly, the standard old-fashioned marriage offered stability. It offered a clearly and unequivocally defined role for the man and one for the woman. They each did their part, and they raised their children confidently — and indeed unquestioningly — in the same way. They knew what they had to do, and they accepted their obligations to each other. Yet, in another sense, at least by contemporary standards of male roles and female roles, mom and dad operated within the context of a rather rigid, role-locked relationship. Dad confined himself to certain traditionally defined modes of feeling and action, characteristic of the breadwinner, the boss of the family, and the stiff-upper-lip bulwark of strength. Artistic, musical, creative, emotional pursuits played little or no part in his role definition. Mom had her identity as the mother, housekeeper, nurturer, reliever of pain, and supplier of dad's sex needs.

The kids knew they could usually get around dad's blustering by going to mom, who could manipulate dad into doing what she wanted him to do. She allowed him to think he made all the important decisions, while she pre-programmed them for him. To complement his role as the doer, thinker, and achiever, she found it appropriate to play just a little dumb, just a little scatterbrained, and just a little incompetent with mechanical things.

Although this kind of relationship served certain purposes well, I disagree with those who consider it necessarily superior to male-female relationships of today. Many women today seem to feel a bit guilty about not simulating mom's relationship with dad, or a bit nostalgic about not having the long-term permanence that mom and dad's marriage had, yet many of them have asserted themselves as individuals in relating to their men to a much greater degree than mom would have ever dared. And many men have accepted it and preferred it. Many women have declared their rights to partake of sex and to enjoy it, tossing aside the traditional view of sex for the woman as a "dirty duty."

Many women find themselves in transition with respect to some of these values, and many men do too. Just during the decade of the 1970s, there has emerged the notion of a love relationship between a man and a woman as a mutual growth proposition, with opportunities for each of them to actualize important values, to grow and to learn, and to pursue lines of self-development, within the context of an affectionate and emotionally supportive relationship. This new view recognizes that people sometimes grow in different directions and at different speeds. For more and more people, the idea of gracefully disengaging from a love relationship when it no longer meets their primary needs seems like a reasonable and mature option rather than a failure. To the extent that they continue to meet their needs by getting along with each other in special ways, while having the freedom to meet other needs in other contexts, they want to continue with their love relationships. When they cannot, they see breaking up as a sensible and mature option, enabling both of them to go ahead in their own ways.

Of course, more times than not only one of the parties decides that he or she can't get the satisfactions necessary for continuing, while the other still wants to continue. If one or both of them have the same highly dependent view of love relationships discussed previously, breaking up can cause them both a great deal of upset and unhappiness. However, the person who can accept and adapt reasonably well tends to look back on his or her love relationships with fond memories rather than with feelings of resentment and disappointment.

Unless you believe in the "one and only" theory of love relationships, which says you will someday meet that one magic person destined to become your life's partner, and you go along waiting for the bells to ring, it makes sense to get involved actively with members of the opposite sex. It makes sense to have a good time with various people, and to choose those for special relationships with whom you feel you can actualize most of your primary needs and values most of the time. Holding back in getting to know someone because you think they won't really qualify as the one and only, or because it probably won't lead to marriage, can limit your happiness for a long time and deprive you of a lot of good times with some interesting people. If you have a clear idea of what you want for your own life, and if you know how to communicate with another person adaptively and assertively within the context of a love relationship, good relationships don't merely happen to you — you make them happen.

sexuality

Anthropologists almost unanimously agree in classifying human beings as the sexiest creatures on earth. They have no mating season but stay sexually active the whole year around. Pregnant females still desire and accept males until late in pregnancy. A significant amount of human communication, both nonverbal and abstract, centers on sex and sexual activity. Paradoxically, only human beings seem to suffer guilt feelings about their sexual behavior. If we consider humans merely well-developed animals, cursed with the faculty of abstract thought, we can make more sense out of our sexual behavior.

Certainly our abstract values, and especially religious values, modulate our sexual behavior. But for many people, sexuality entails an inordinate degree of uncertainty, guilt, apprehension, and conflict. One can deny his or her sexuality on an intellectual level, but not on a physical level. The body has its appetites, and it transmits its messages to the brain. The owner of the body can either acknowledge and accept this sexual function, or can block it off from awareness and conscious processing. His or her behavior will clearly express the choice he or she has made.

The "sexual revolution" has its positive side as well as its regressive side. An analysis of this phenomenon lies far beyond our purposes here, but it does make sense for us to examine the issue of acceptance of one's sexuality, because it plays such an important part in one's physical and psychological well-being and one's happiness level.

Many people underestimate the importance of an effective sexual adjustment, especially in marriage, for example. Some marriage counsellors and therapists estimate that at least fifty percent of married couples have relatively dysfunctional sexual relationships, which means that they do not regularly enjoy having intercourse together as a mutually pleasurable activity. This seems to stem from at least two factors: conflicting feelings and attitudes created by early childhood programming, and ineptness or inexperience at the intimate communication process which enables both people to enjoy making love.

The traditional Victorian programming which established the basic sexual attitudes of many over-thirty adults has recently begun to fade, and more and more young adults consider sex a form of fulfillment for woman and man alike. But many women past the age of about thirty grew up with a fairly standard definition of sex as a wifely duty, a male privilege built into the institution of marriage, and a way to make babies. In years past, people considered a woman who actually enjoyed sex and sought sexual gratification from her husband a bit perverted and lacking in the feminine traits a good wife should have. Males, for the most part, grew up with the notion of sexual intercourse as a form of dominance over a female. Sex outside of a marital relationship amounted to "scoring" on a woman, who traded her sexual favors for whatever he offered in return. Sex within a marital or premarital relationship amounted to a special privilege, which the woman could bestow more or less at discretion, but with some sense of eventual obligation. Many men and women still have essentially this view of the interpersonal dynamics of sex, or at least traces of it.

Recently, however, sex without marriage has emerged as an acceptable social value, as witnessed by the number of couples living together, the common practice of single people dating and staying the night with each other, taking trips and staying in hotels together, and making love on the first or second date. Some people older than about thirty still have trouble adjusting to this style of living, but many younger people see it as quite normal and acceptable. Many of them view sex as not essentially connected to marriage, although necessary for a successful marriage.

Regardless of your religious persuasion or your social values with respect to sexual intercourse, the definition of personal effectiveness that forms the foundation of this book entails a straightforward acknowledgement and acceptance of your sexuality, as an important physical aspect of your functioning. Whatever the "rules" you impose on sexual activity for yourself, you cannot function as a completely self-actualizing human being while suppressing or denying your sexual impulses as a general policy.

Accepting your sexuality means several things. First, it means recognizing when you feel sexually attracted to someone, whether or not you intend to follow up on the attraction. By simply acknowledging your appetite, you affirm yourself as a completely functioning human. Second, it means actively engaging in sexual intercourse with a person of your choosing, within the context of a relationship that aligns with your other personal values. Here, allow me to accept responsibility explicitly for this bias — the notion that every human being needs, wants, and deserves at least occasional sexual gratification with another human being; not everyone would necessarily accept this notion, but I consider it fundamental.

Third, accepting your sexuality means the capacity to enjoy sexual intercourse, not merely accept it or tolerate it for some "higher" purpose associated with the other person. It means relinquishing childhood-derived apprehensions and attitudes of distaste and acquiring a certain earthy, physical orientation to your body — looking at it, acknowledging it, respecting it, and approving of it. It also means learning to make love *with* someone, not *to* them, or worse, *at* them. It means accepting intercourse as the most intimate act of human communication, as well as just plain fun.

negotiating and contracting

Managing love relationships requires, as we say, "give and take." Two people will only stay together and continue to get along well with each other so long as *both* of them find substantial need-satisfaction and actualization of their primary values. This seems obvious to some people, and it escapes others entirely. If you want to continue getting along well with your partner, you'll have to continually tend to the matter of mutual need-satisfaction, not just to satisfying your own needs and not just to satisfying the other person's needs.

Actually, a policy of "positive selfishness" tends to work out for the best. Instead of trying to second-guess the other person's needs and values, and having him or her try to second-guess yours, it makes more sense to tend to your own needs and values carefully, and to expect the other person to tend carefully to his or hers. If you both do this, then you both know what issues you have to tend to, what problems you want to solve, and what corrections you want to make. It tends to make the communication process quite efficient.

You need two basic skills, or processes, to balance the "costs" and "benefits" fairly for both people in a love relationship. You need the skill of *negotiating*, or bargaining and compromising to get what you want while helping the other person get what he or she wants. And you need the skill of *contracting*, or making explicit agreements about behavior and expectations. Negotiating and contracting, when practiced by both parties, tend to eliminate or avoid confusion and hard feelings associated with unspoken expectations and implied obligations. If you don't like some aspect of the other person's behavior, don't bludgeon him or her with your expectations. Instead, try for an explicit contract, an agreement about what he or she will do in certain circumstances, and what you will do in return. Then you both have the right to hold certain expectations, because you've mutually agreed to them. For your own part, you don't allow the other person to push you this way or that, in the name of unspecified or implied "responsibilities." You abide by the expectations you've agreed to.

Especially in preparation for marriage, or a live-together arrangement, two people can negotiate and contract with each other to eliminate a host of misunderstandings and surprises downstream. Of course, if either or both of them prefer a power struggle to a mature and adaptive relationship, then negotiating and contracting will not seem very attractive to them. But, for those who want to deal with each other on an adaptive, assertive, value-confirming, and need-satisfying basis, the following process can work very well:

1. Take a pen and paper and itemize your key wants; what aspects of your own life and behavior do you hold sacred? What specific activities, processes, habits, possessions, and interactions do you consider beyond the range of compromise? Which others do you consider important, but open to negotiation? Ask your prospective partner to do the same. Consider as many variables as you can think of: time structuring, sex, social activities, friends and acquaintances, parents, hobbies and recreation, where to live, money, travel, careers, children, and so on. Anything you hold back or conceal at this point will probably rise to haunt you later.

2. Exchange lists and study them.

3. Identify potentially conflicting values or objectives.

4. Work out a compromise in each major area, in *specific* behavioral terms. What can you expect of the other person, and what will you agree to have him or her expect of you? Avoid terms like "be considerate" and stick to behaviorally recognizable items like "call me and let me know whether you plan to come home at a certain time."

5. Spell out your agreement in so many words; what have you agreed to do, and what has he or she agreed to do? Write it down in simple form, make a copy for each of you, and tuck it away somewhere after memorizing it.

6. When problems or misunderstandings arise, invoke the contract. Haul it out and remind yourselves what you agreed to. If the agreement no longer seems feasible, go back to the negotiating and bargaining process, and make a new contract. If you find the two of you "can't" or won't negotiate and establish contracts any longer, then consider breaking up. You've probably got a well-developed, no-win power struggle instead of a rewarding love relationship. So long as you can identify issues, negotiate, and contract, you can communicate adaptively, and you can continue with a love relationship as a process of mutual need-satisfaction.

IV

GETTING ALONG IN GROUPS

15

HOW PEOPLE BEHAVE IN TASK GROUPS

Extending our study of the competence category of social competence as an important element of personal effectiveness, we can now explore the matter of getting what we want by constructive strategies within group situations. Here we enter the interesting realm of *group dynamics*, the study of the ways in which a person's perception of himself as a member of a well-defined group influences his behavior.

Since we focus in this book on the adult, professional, career-oriented person, we will deal primarily with working situations, that is, *task groups*. In simple terms, we will consider a task group as a relatively small group of people who have some common job to do, or who have to work more or less cooperatively to get something done. This excludes the interesting but remotely related study of behavior in purely social settings, bus-stop behavior, crowd behavior, and the like. Here we focus on the behavior of our working colleagues — and ourselves — in fairly typical business situations.

recognizing structure and process in a group situation

When a typical task group convenes to do business, either on a one-time special basis or as part of an on-going pattern of working, most of the group members will slip immediately and quite unconsciously into certain well-defined behavior patterns which they have learned to identify as appropriate "member behavior." They will usually begin working on the item of business at hand, paying little or no attention to the more subtle aspects of the overall group process. Most of them become completely preoccupied with their own individual parts of the task and with proceeding with the immediate business.

As an observer, you can identify two distinct levels of human interaction in a task situation, both of which you can profitably study and monitor while you play your particular part. Let's call them *content* and *context* and define them as follows:

1. *Content* — the readily perceived level of concrete activity, directed toward the overtly specified purposes of the group. This may include discussing a particular topic, carrying out a physical activity such as making or assembling something, taking turns reporting on various topics, or working together to solve a problem or make a decision. The content of the situation involves the particulars of the members' activity — the basic elements or work associated directly with the performance of the task.

2. *Context* — the abstractly defined and

abstractly perceived level of human *processes*, which transcend the performance of this particular task or the solving of this particular problem and which characterize human task-group behavior in general. The context of the situation deals with the "how" of the group's activity rather than the "what." It involves group norms, interpersonal influence, authority factors, information exchange processes, task procedures, decision processes, and the interpersonal relationships and transactions peculiar to the specific individuals present.

In any human interaction, and indeed across an entire culture, some things get communicated explicitly by consciously directed messages, while others get communicated implicitly by the very setting itself, and by people's habits, traditions, expectations, nonverbal actions, and reactions. This happens in a task group as well. Some important things go on at the level of content, that is, the task activities, and other important things go on at the context level, or the more abstract level of processes. So we can also call these the levels of *task* and *process*, or the *explicit* and *implicit* levels, respectively.

Behavioral scientists refer to the skill of observing these context-level processes as *process awareness*. To have a highly developed process awareness means that you can mentally step back from your own involvement in the details of the paticular situation and tune in to the higher level social processes going on within the group, some of which will involve you. Relatively few people seem to have developed this skill very highly, as witness the number of times that task groups get caught in procedural tangles, interpersonal conflicts, and factional differences, with the members unable to realize what has happened to them and unable to find a path out of the woods. If you have developed a high level of process awareness, you can not only play your own part more effectively, but you can achieve your own individual purposes more readily, and you can also exert a certain degree of strategic influence over the affairs of the group. If the other members have little or no awareness of the context level, and get stuck at the level of particulars, you can examine the happenings from the point of view of the group's overall purposes, and you can intervene tactfully, constructively, and influentially to help them get moving in a productive direction again.

Developing process awareness means knowing what to look for. In observing the group's functioning at the process level, you can spot:

1. Authority and influence among the various individuals.
2. Relative degree of individuals' participation, ranging from very active to "dropped out."
3. Interactions between particular individuals, either productive or problematical.

any work group has certain distinctive interaction processes, which transcend the task itself

4. Flow of information; who has it and what they do with it.
5. Specific task procedures and the extent to which they help or hinder the group.
6. Decision processes, decision awareness, role of formal authority.
7. Consensus-making and consensus-testing.
8. Controversy; tolerance of diverse viewpoints.
9. Psychological tone, or "mood," of the group; social norms; effects of physical setting.
10. Group's progress with the task; degree to which members proceed smoothly.

As a group leader, either formally appointed or informally selected, or as a highly aware group member, you can more or less continuously monitor this process level and identify any blocks to the group's progress. You can use this knowledge to make yourself valuable to the group, and therefore maximally influential.

formal authority and "earned" authority

If you take a close look, you'll find that virtually every stable task group you can find has a relatively well-defined structure to its operation, and it has a well-defined authority function. No task group can function very well for very long without someone "in charge." This statement says more about human desires for structure and social order than it says about matters of efficiency. Having someone in charge and having a properly distributed "pecking order" seem absolutely fundamental to human cooperative interaction.

Think about this in any context you choose; classrooms, business organizations, baseball teams, military units, governments, crews travelling to the moon. Human beings sooner or later establish a predictable structure and order to their activities. In any group situation, the members tend to settle the matter of authority, either formal or informal, before dealing with any operational matters. As things go along, they will reaffirm the authority structure as needed, and they will usually give it the very highest priority when it appears to need attention. If you fully grasp the significance of this fact, you can understand group dynamics fairly readily, and you can operate much more effectively in group situations than most other people can.

One simple model of group processes, which can help you observe the happenings and put them into perspective, deals with the stages a group goes through, usually unconsciously, in stabilizing itself and becoming a functioning task unit. Starting with a group of people who haven't previously worked together as a task group on some particular matter at hand, we can trace out four stages:

1. *Forming* — assembling themselves in one place, such as a conference room or in a general work area, and identifying themselves as members of a group with some well-defined common purpose; deciding who "belongs" to the group and who doesn't; drawing specific dividing lines and criteria to. define group membership.

2. *Storming* — working out a satisfactory pattern of roles and forms of influence; the group's "politics," which determines the relative amounts of authority and influence various members have; possibly acknowledging a formal leader appointed by a higher authority, electing a formal leader, or accepting the emergence of a *de facto* leader.

3. *Norming* — setting conscious or implied standards of individual behavior which the group members expect of each other; developing or assuming a code of ethics; establishing social protocol; formulating or adopting a set of group values which will guide the behavior of the members, and to which the members at large will adhere in countering "deviant" behavior by one or more individual members.

4. *Performing* — turning their attention fully to the work they have to do and settling into modes of working that seem to meet the needs of the situation; relying on the previously established authority pattern and the accepted norms of behavior to give structure to their interactions and to guide them in dealing with one another.

Since most people approach new task situations with their attention almost solely on the task itself, these four stages usually proceed unconsciously, or semiconsciously at most. If the group members get stuck at one stage, they usually can't proceed very effectively to the next one. For example, unless they settle the basic issues of the storming stage, they will probably have a great deal of trouble parceling up the work and compromising in getting it done in the performing stage.

Similarly, if the group has some unresolved "norm" problems, such as status differences among members which entitle some to greater acceptance of their ideas than others, they will have to overcome those in order to function effectively at the performing stage. This might happen, for example, in a mixed-gender group, where the men do not accord the women full status as influential parties in making certain decisions. If the women refuse to accept this one-down status, the subsequent cooperation will probably suffer.

In each case, when a problem arises associated with inadequate resolution of one of the stages, the group members will find themselves pulled backward toward that particular stage. If they try to ignore the issues, which many people do in groups, they will at best settle for some less effective mode of working at the performing level.

As a group member, you can use your process observation skills to trace the group's progress, or lack of it, through these four stages. If you can identify the snags they might have encountered in developing their processes, you can intervene constructively to get them going again. The key to gaining influence in a group lies in coming up with just the right intervention, as the following section explains.

Regardless of whether the group has accepted you or appointed you as their formal leader, you can develop a degree of de facto leadership, or informal influence in its affairs. By using positive, adaptive, and assertive communication techniques, you can earn the respect, trust, and willingness to cooperate of most of the group members, Indeed, we can call this a form of "earned" authority. As an individual member, you therefore have two possible kinds of authority:

1. *Formal authority* — the recognized right to lead the group in various activities; either acquired from a higher formal authority, or accorded to you by consensus of the group, it entitles you to make certain decisions, instruct members to do various things, and to organize and coordinate their activities.

2. *Earned authority* — the sum total of the interpersonal authority accorded to you by the individuals of the group; based on the degree to which they feel positively disposed toward you,

they will look to you for influence at various strategic times, and they will accept a certain amount of direction from you.

This dual-authority concept opens up some interesting possibilities for understanding the "real life" leadership processes in a group, rather than getting stuck in theoretical formulations. It enables you to assess all of the influence patterns in the group, not just those revolving around the formal leader. If we define leadership rather loosely, as simply a matter of getting others to do what you want them to do, then we can see the significance of blending the effects of formal and informal authority.

For example, you've probably participated in situations where the person with high formal authority also enjoyed high earned authority with group members, and consequently had maximal influence in their processes. Conversely, you've probably seen people with high formal authority who so undermined themselves with toxic interpersonal styles that they developed very little earned authority, or you might even say they had "negative" earned authority, which offset their formal authority. You might also have seen a person with little or no formal authority, but with high earned authority, become more influential overall with group members than the formal leader who had much less earned authority. And, of course, at the extreme end of the scale we have the person with no formal authority and negative earned authority, who lives in continual jeopardy of getting expelled from the group.

Rather than get tangled up in theoretical formulations of the abstract concept of "leadership," just think in terms of your total influence in a situation as the extent to which you can get others to do what you want them to do. It goes without saying, of course, that you have to meet certain of their needs and values in order to influence their behavior. Whatever combination of formal authority and earned authority you've developed enables you to do this.

distributed leadership: the locus of influence

If you've participated in many group situations, you've almost certainly seen a situation in which an individual tries to "take over" the group in an early and aggressive bid to become the most influential person. You may have seen someone succeed at this, and you may also have seen someone fail clumsily, with the group clearly rejecting his or her bid for the de facto role of boss. Have you wondered about the difference? Why did one person make it, while the other one flopped? If you know the answer to this question, in the general sense, you can develop your "take-over" skills to a high degree. You can equip yourself to go into a task group and emerge as one of the most influential people there, and you can have a strong directing effect on its processes, if you choose to do so. You may or may not want to do this on many occasions, but it helps to know how. It also helps to know how to *avoid* having the group put you in the high influence role if you don't want it.

The aggressive take-over person usually doesn't realize that only certain behaviors will actually gain recognition by group members as leading behaviors. When he tries too hard to take over, he loses sight of the key factor: the *usefulness to the group* of his action. He doesn't have a clear idea of what to propose and what not to, and particularly when. By developing this "what-and-when" sensitivity, you can emerge with a high influence role without any kind of an interpersonal struggle.

Five kinds of process-level "interventions," corresponding to five kinds of snags a group might encounter, can equip you to help the group further its purposes and get rolling again whenever it has difficulty. Whenever you provide one of these "unblocking" suggestions or actions, group members consciously or unconsciously recognize it as helpful to the group's overall purposes, and they mentally add a point to your score as an influential person. These five kinds of interventions correspond to the following five aspects of group process:

1. *Task* — anything you do to contribute directly to the accomplishment of the work at hand; helping with the work, showing a new or better way, or getting rid of obstacles to someone else's effective performance.

2. *Procedure* — the most common snag in meeting situations; suggesting that the group reconsider the procedure they've adopted for dealing with the task, suggesting alternative procedures, or suggesting that they adopt an explicit procedure where none seems to exist; inviting them to pay attention to *how* they do what they do, how they organize themselves, how they allocate resources, how they schedule their time, how they structure their interactions.

3. *Information* — anything you do to improve the availability of useful information to group members; giving information, taking action to get it, inviting group members to share what they know, suggesting ways in which members can generate, pool, process, and distribute information important to getting the task done.

4. *Decisions* — inviting the group's attention to various decision issues; helping them structure decision processes, analyze problems and arrive at decisions; inviting them to think about

how to decide as well as what to decide about; helping others to share in the decision process, rather than trying to dominate it or trying to push one preferred solution.

5. *Social stability* — any constructive action you take to reduce conflict, help clear up controversy, ease tension, promote better rapport among group members, and help individuals join in the mainstream of the group's activity.

If you'd like to develop your skills at earning authority in group situations, try the following process. When you next sit down with a task group to which you belong, wait a few minutes for the group to get going in some direction or other. Observe their processes carefully. If some aggressive individual attempts a take-over, just sit quietly; resist the urge to counter his influence. As you observe the group moving along some particular line of action, sooner or later — probably sooner — they will hit a snag. Two members might disagree and get into a shouting match, the group might have an unrecognized problem with missing or misleading information, they might waste too much time in some unproductive activity, they might get tangled up in a decision issue, or they might have trouble with some particular thing they want to do at the moment. Each of these snags provides you with an opportunity for an *appropriate intervention* into the group's process — a chance to unblock the flow of useful activity. By diagnosing the snag as one of the five categories listed above, you can come up with a suggestion or an action that solves the snag. Whereas the take-over person simply tries to get his hands on the steering wheel by a direct lunge, you acquire a de facto steering wheel by having the group members award it to you for making useful contributions. This underscores the tremendous importance of the process observation skill.

If you watch the goings-on in a task group from the point of view of these five categories of interaction, task, procedure, information, decisions, and social stability, you can watch the "instantaneous leadership" function shift from one person to another. This makes clear that no group has only one leader, but that each member offers leading behavior to some degree. Some offer a great deal of influence, some offer very little; most fall somewhere in the middle. This notion of *distributed leadership* enables you to "watch the action" as things proceed and to watch the pattern by which momentary influence shifts from person to person. We can refer to the "path" travelled by the influence function from moment to moment as the *locus of influence*, and we can even diagram it. You could make a sketch of the seating arrangement and draw arrows to show who had the ball and who got it next. And you would find that having the ball in the vast majority of cases involved one or more of the five aspects of group interaction enumerated above.

assessing your interaction style

You have to decide for yourself how you want to deal with the matter of interpersonal influence, and especially influence in groups. If you consider yourself a shy, underassertive person, and you dislike the whole idea of trying to influence other people, consider the fact that influence always exists, including the influences other people have on you. You can't realistically expect to escape from human politics; it exists in all group situations.

If you assess your interaction style as somewhat underassertive in group situations, and you think you would profit by developing your leadership skills, you will probably first have to solve the problem of underassertiveness. By studying the concepts of self-esteem and assertive communication covered previously, you can work out a self-change plan focused on the specific behaviors of appropriate intervention described in the preceding section.

You can also use the shy person's technique of *graduated behavior programming*, in which you progressively assert yourself more and more, using behaviors chosen as low-risk "starters." For example, you might start by simply training yourself to speak up in group meetings. Lay claim to your fair share of "air time," and don't cop out on yourself with the excuse "But I really don't have anything to say most of the time." If you find it too scary to give your ideas, start by just asking questions, a much lower risk form of behavior. Then you can proceed to using questions to make other people reconsider key issues and to direct their attention where you want it. Conversely, if you consider yourself overassertive, and perhaps a bit of a bull in the china shop in group settings, train yourself to reduce your use of air time, even lower than your fair share, and confine your interventions to carefully chosen unblocking actions. Step back more often and pay attention to the group's processes, keep your ego under control, and match your actions to the needs of the situation as it unfolds.

DEVELOPING YOUR MANAGEMENT SKILLS

do you want
a management job?

Most professional people who work in organizational settings sooner or later come face to face with the possibility of "getting into management." Some get interested in the potential challenges of a management job, some just get curious about it, and some have the possibility suddenly thrust upon them. Many people with technical specialties reach a career stage where they find less satisfaction in the details of their work, and they want some kind of a change. For them, a management job seems intriguing. If you face such a situation currently, you might want to think long and carefully about the ramifications of this major change in your career.

Most business organizations have only the most rudimentary processes for identifying potential new managers, training them, preparing them for their jobs, and placing them properly. Most have no particular system for assessing managerial performance and for rescuing the failing manager and minimizing the hardship to the people he manages. This leads to a very common organizational syndrome, that of the unqualified specialist-turned-manager. Typically, a person will distinguish himself as a practitioner of some specialty, for example, cost accounting, field sales, or nursing. When the job of group supervisor opens up, someone in upper management will tag this specialist-expert as the logical choice for the job. The manager reasons that "Mary really knows nursing, so she would logically make the best head nurse." Or, the reasoning goes, "Jack has been in engineering for twenty years. He really knows heat-exchanger design. He's the logical guy to head up the heat-exchanger design group." If Mary or Jack don't have the social competence needed to deal effectively with the other people in the group, and if they don't understand the functional role of a manager, no amount of nursing or engineering experience will make up for it.

If you haven't had any direct experience at supervising others, or if you feel you lack some of the important skills needed to do well at a managerial job, think the matter over carefully. Don't allow yourself to get thrown into a managerial job without adequate preparation; it can easily damage your career, and at the very least put you through some trying experiences. If you see a promotion into management in the offing, and if you feel you'd like to try it, then begin immediately to get the training and preparation necessary for it. Go to the training department and arrange to take a basic course in management *before* they throw you into the water. Find out what things you'll have to do and what problems you'll have to face when you first get into the job, and get ready for them.

Even if you don't see a promotion in the immediate future, and you feel you'd like to try your hand at management, you can still do the same things to prepare. At the very least, take a good course in management and read a few of the contemporary books on various aspects of human relations, communication, and applied behavioral sciences. When your time comes, make sure you can go into the new situation with the odds on your side.

the "new manager" syndrome

Most people who go into management jobs do survive the experience, and most of them do reasonably well at it over the long run. A few, of course, make excellent managers, and a few make lousy managers. A large fraction of new managers, in any case, find the experience more difficult and traumatic than necessary, because they haven't prepared for it well, and because they don't know how to overcome their own anxieties and direct their energies positively during the critical first few weeks and months of their new jobs.

For probably eighty percent of inexperienced first-time managers, fear presents the biggest obstacle — fear of failing, fear of looking incompetent or foolish, and fear of not having the skills to cope with unforeseen and unknown problems which might arise. For them, making the transition into the new job becomes an unconscious race between education and catastrophe. Unfortunately, too many new managers react to these feelings of insecurity and apprehension with counterproductive ego-building tactics in dealing with the people they supervise. Many a new manager finds himself thrown into the job unprepared, feels anxious and insecure, and suddenly turns grim, over-serious, and abrasive in his interpersonal dealings with subordinates.

While trying to escape from the feeling of insecurity, he may inadvertently destroy his most valuable resource — the good will of the people whom he now must manage. By trying to cover up his fear and apprehensions with an air of false bravado, he oppresses and intimidates his staff members, cuts them down, undermines their own sense of security, and loses all or most of his earned authority. Relatively few new managers catch on to the basic trick of becoming a manager painlessly, namely establishing rapport and a mutually supportive relationship with the people they manage. In their preoccupation with fear of failure, they overlook the most important factor in success.

Unfortunately, too many managers never learn to overcome their fear of failing, and they may continue for years in a toxic and self-defeating behavior pattern. They develop permanent myopia about their repulsive behavior and their lack of earned authority, and they learn to rationalize their behavior with statements like "These people are just lazy," or "You have to keep after people to get the work out of them," and, of course, the classic: "You just can't get good people these days."

This syndrome of the "maladjusted manager," that is, one who never came to terms with his own fears and his own need for ego-gratification, occurs with discouraging frequency in business organizations. When it happens, the organization loses in human productivity; the people lose in morale, esprit de corps, and quality of work life; and even the manager loses. Yet few organizations have a definite system for rescuing or removing the maladjusted manager and moving him back into some line of work he *can* do well, and consequently improving the psychological lot of the staff members. Toxic, maladjusted first-line supervisors probably play the most important role in driving the employees of a company into the arms of a labor union.

If you want to avoid becoming the classic maladjusted manager, and make your learning process relatively painless, keep these pointers in mind:

1. Don't fake it; don't pretend to know what you don't know, and don't pretend to understand what you don't understand; ask questions and learn.

2. Don't confuse your ego with your authority; use your authority straightforwardly and without apologizing for it, but use it sparingly and gracefully.

3. Get help; form a "mentor" relationship with an experienced manager, a consultant, a management trainer, or a personnel officer; call on expert advice and temper your thinking with a more seasoned view.

4. Establish rapport with the members of your staff and keep it; protect it, defend it, and nurture it; look out for them and they'll look out for you.

four dimensions of managerial competence

In thinking about a managerial job, it helps to have some simple model, or systematic framework for describing and assessing the competencies needed to do well. You can make sense of the job of manager, in virtually any organization, by considering it to have four distinct dimensions, defined by the following behavioral roles:

1. *Strategist* — one who thinks about the overall purposes of the group, the "grand design"; you must get a clear

idea of the important purposes of the group, look at the disparities between what the group accomplishes and what it should accomplish, reflect on the future, and begin preparing for the changes and trends you see there.

2. *Leader* — one who clearly and unequivocally shows the members of the group the necessary direction, helps them understand and accept it, and helps them work effectively toward it; here you must set goals, often by consultation and cooperation with group members; you must give the necessary instruction and you must provide the encouragement, positive feedback, and material and psychological rewards commensurate with results; you must also help group members grow in their jobs and develop their capabilities and their careers.

3. *Problem-solver* — one who enables group members to deal effectively with obstacles and to exploit upcoming opportunities effectively and efficiently; you must support, assist, advise, and encourage them in dealing with the new and unfamiliar situations, and you must help them develop new strategies and find new and better ways to achieve worthwhile results; you must make decisions effectively, you must innovate, and you must teach others to innovate.

4. *Administrator* — one who develops useful, simple, effective, and efficient systems and methods which help group members maximize their productive results; here you must make plans, organize and assign people and skills to various result areas, monitor progress and measure results, and streamline procedures to minimize wasted effort and maximize accomplishment.

assessing
your managerial skills

Since you'll need to have a variety of special skills to do well in your new job of manager, or at least to demonstrate the competence that will invite upper management to give you a chance at it, you can plan and guide your learning process most effectively by making a realistic assessment of your present skills. Even without a great deal of familiarity with the overall field of management, you can still make a reasonable preliminary estimate in order to get started with your program of skill-development.

Using the four managerial roles discussed in the preceding section, strategist, leader, problem-solver, and administrator, you can begin to reflect on the specific kinds of things you'll have to do in a managerial job. Try taking a pen and paper and making a "forced-choice" ranking of these four roles in terms of your own perception of your competence right now. From highest to lowest, and granting no ties, how would you rank them for yourself? What specific factors did you consider in arriving at this assessment?

With some particular kind of work unit in mind, such as you might conceivably manage, just put your feet up and think as concretely as you can about the kinds of things you'll need to accomplish in each of the four areas. Think about other managers you've seen in similar jobs. What did they do? What things dominated their time? How effectively do you feel they handled their jobs? What mistakes did they make that you can learn to avoid? Think about the day-to-day flow of events you might experience.

As you think about various aspects of the job, at least as well as you can picture it, make note of the kinds of capabilities you want to improve on. Write these items down and use them as a personal agenda in working your way through a management training program. Make sure the training experience meets your needs, and make sure you explore those areas more fully that have special importance for you.

MANAGING A GROUP
OF PEOPLE
EFFECTIVELY

enabling people
vs. commanding them

Management as an institutional role seems to have become progressively less authoritarian over the past ten to twenty years, and a good deal more humanistic. While many older managers, brought up and socialized in a pre-war era of authoritarian boss-employee relationships, still tend toward the distant, rigid, one-way pattern of directing people and communicating instructions to them, many younger managers and some older ones have gravitated more and more toward a participative philosophy.

We can think of this shift in terms of two polarities on a continuum scale, with the *commander* style at one end and the *enabler* style at the other, as illustrated by Figure 17–1. The traditional commander style involves a general one-way flow of instructions from manager to employee, on a rather elemental level rather than in terms of objectives. The commander tends to give orders in bits and pieces, on a day-to-day or even moment-to-moment basis. He takes responsibility for virtually all of the thinking processes, for setting the goals and performance targets, and also for deciding how the employees should do the work. This style focuses on *work* rather than on *results*.

THE "COMMANDER"

Directs
Controls
Tells
Punishes

THE "ENABLER"

Shares Goals
Delegates
Guides
Motivates
Rewards

fig. 17-1: modern management requires an "enabling" style more than a "commanding" one

The enabler style, on the other hand, starts with the notion that the employee should direct his own work to the greatest feasible extent, freeing him from the step-by-step control of the manager, and freeing the manager for the other roles of strategist, problem-solver, and administrator. The enabler tends to communicate with employees in terms of large-scale results, or *objectives*, and to delegate whole tasks or projects to them for completion largely as they see fit. This more flexible style makes much more sense these days, and especially in the kinds of work environments we have in modern organizations.

a model of leadership style

In keeping with the behavioral approach to personal effectiveness we've adopted in this book, let's look at leadership as an important part of the competence category of social competence. Let's model the *enabling* leadership style in terms of four categories of managerial behavior:

1. *Shared goals* — you maintain a give-and-take relationship with your staff members, sharing ideas, information, perceptions of problems and issues, and possibilities for solving them. When you establish goals for the group to work for, you do so as a result of a well-thought-out problem-solving process. By accounting for their views and interests in setting goals, you give them a stake in the goals, and you make it more likely that they will support them and work in a self-motivated way to achieve them. Although you retain the responsibility for setting goals and performance standards, you enable the employees to participate constructively in the process.

2. *Teamwork* — you use periodic group activities, staff meetings, and group problem-solving sessions as a way to build a sense of group identity and team spirit, while accomplishing worthwhile results. By using meetings and conferences sparingly but strategically, you can balance individual work with group work and maximize the sense of team effectiveness. You can also encourage, by example and by instruction, a process of sharing ideas and information, helping one another with overloads and unforeseen problems, and resolving controversies by cooperation and compromise.

3. *Autonomy* — you grant to each individual on your staff a degree of freedom of action appropriate to his or her experience and level of maturity, and the task or mission area involved. You grant them the freedom to learn, to make mistakes, and to accomplish results using their own imagination and ingenuity, to the maximum feasible extent, commensurate with the group's goals. You give close guidance and support to those who need it most, and you give "running room" to those who have shown they can handle it responsibly. You delegate work in terms of whole tasks or projects whenever possible, enabling the employee to experience the psychological sense of *closure* associated with seeing a task through to completion.

4. *Reward* — you provide feedback, honest praise and compliments, formal recognition of achievement, and salary compensation commensurate with results. You deal with people in a nourishing, attractive, affirmative interpersonal style, using your status and authority as manager to reward them psychologically for working effectively. You don't "overdo" praise and rewards, thereby diminishing

the significance of them; and you don't "underdo" it either, thereby making employees feel used and unappreciated. You match recognition and rewards — both material and psychological — to achievement.

By combining these four categories of action in a mixture appropriate to the people and the situation, you tend to liberate them and enable them to do their best. You build morale, team spirit, commitment to results, and respect and loyalty to you as a leader. You maximize your earned authority, largely by deploying your formal authority effectively and gracefully, and by challenging people to achieve and develop.

managing by objectives

The subject of *objectives* deserves special attention with respect to the topic of management. Not all managers understand clearly the crucial importance of having their employees understand the big picture. Some content themselves with the traditional commander style of supervision, with little regard for the employees' comprehension of or commitment to the higher purpose.

If you want to manage effectively, you'll have to train yourself to think again and again in terms of objectives. Why do we do what we do? What ultimate purposes do we serve? What constitutes "payoff" in our particular corner of the world? How do we know when we've done well? How do we measure effectiveness in our pursuits? You can't possibly hope to show your employees where they should go if you don't know yourself.

Reflect back on the ideas in Chapter 7, with respect to setting personal goals. If you've developed the habit of thinking, planning, and acting in terms of goals in your personal life, you'll find it a simple matter to extend that approach to a managerial job. Thinking in terms of goals will enable you to pay attention to what really counts, to prioritize, and to focus your energies for maximum benefit to your organization, your work group, and yourself. Try reading one of the many useful books available devoted to the philosophy of *management by objectives*.* Don't mistake the *concept* of management by objectives for some kind of a paper system. Think of it as a style, a philosphy, and a behavioral approach, rather than a method. Begin to make the strategies

Successful Management by Objectives: An Action Manual by Karl Albrecht (Englewood Cliffs, N.J.: Prentice-Hall, Inc., 1978), now in its sixth printing, gives a thorough treatment of the concepts and techniques used in the management-by-objectives approach and shows how to apply it in various organizations.

associated with management by objectives a regular part of your thinking process, and incorporate them in your dealings with your employees.

building a team

If you'd like to have a fairly simple "recipe" for building an effective team, keep three words in mind: goals, roles, and plans. By combining these three critical elements, and by adding a little imagination, some adaptability, and a practical turn of mind, you can organize a group of people effectively and you can lead them to accomplish worthwhile results while they gain personal satisfaction in doing so.

With respect to *goals*, or objectives, your leader role involves setting a clear sense of direction for the group, expressing that direction in the form of specific, measurable, practical, achievable, and worthwhile objectives, and then guiding the efforts of the team members in a general way to achieve them.

The concept of *roles* can help you enormously in allocating your human resources, motivating and rewarding people, and maintaining an orderly work process. Just as the members of a baseball team have their own individual areas of action and responsibility, so you can divide the result areas of the group into specific roles which you can assign to various members. When a person has a consistent, long-term definition of the part he should play on the team, analogous to playing second base, he can organize his work and his own developmental efforts more effectively than if the boss shifts him around without rhyme or reason. Not everyone gets to do everything he wants, and everyone occasionally has to take on something he or she wouldn't necessarily prefer. But, over the long run, you as the manager can define and clarify various roles for members of the group, aligned with their result areas, and you can lend a useful and logical pattern to their interactions.

And, finally, have a *plan*. Clarify the group's overall undertaking for the next quarter, or six months, or year, and write it down in simple form. Make it brief, concise, and definite. Give each member of the team a copy. Plan the work and then work the plan.

handling controversy
and conflict

Controversy can play a useful, stimulating, and productive part in a team's operation. Honest disagreements, shared forthrightly, analyzed thoroughly, and considered objectively, can help team members broaden their ideas and develop versatile approaches to problems and issues. By keeping the controversy confined to *issues* instead of interpersonal struggles, team members can disagree without fighting. You as a manager can support this process by the way in which you deal with staff members. And you can profit from it by enriching your point of view with the diversity of their ideas.

Conflict, on the other hand, defined as disagreement in which the disagreeing parties fall into a direct adversary relationship, substituting "personalities" for issues, can divide the team into factions, create animosities and misunderstandings, undermine cooperation, and destroy morale. As a manager, you need to systematically track down and eliminate as many of the sources of potential conflict as you can. Encourage healthy controversy, but do not tolerate divisive conflict.

Make sure that you don't inadvertently encourage staff members to fight with one another, by the effects of your actions. Playing favorites, for example, will amost surely pit one person against another eventually. Leaving roles undefined tends to increase confusion and make it more difficult for team members to maintain a habit of cooperation and compromise. Imposing unrealistic demands and creating a punitive atmosphere may cause them to turn against one another as a way to shift the blame or the punishment.

Conversely, maintaining a positive communication atmosphere, modelling and encouraging the behavior pattern of constructive confrontation, treating all members fairly and equitably, and insisting that they confine their disagreements to substantive issues can build a healthy spirit of cooperative problem solving.

allocating your time and energy effectively

If you want to manage effectively, you'll have to make up your mind to manage your job rather than allow it to manage you. So many managers get overwhelmed by the tide of trivia coming at them every day that they never get the upper hand on their jobs, and they never get into the anticipatory mode. They can't get a head start on upcoming issues, because they stay forever in the "crunch mode." They become "fire department" managers. It takes a very aggressive, energetic, and determined approach to get the upper hand on your managerial job and keep it.

To begin with, decide what things you consider truly important in the way of results. Make up your mind what results constitute the real payoffs of your unit, and keep your attention fastened on those areas. Don't let trivia sidetrack you from getting these things accomplished.

Above all, learn to delegate effectively. Think of your job as manager not as a matter of doing the work of the unit, but of getting it done. The members of your unit have to do the work; you have to enable them, help them, and guide them. Keep your mind on the management process, not on the bits and pieces of the day-to-day work. By keeping goals, roles, and plans clearly defined, you help the group members to maximize their collective productivity.

Teach your staff members to think in terms of the big picture — purposes, goals, results, and priorities. Encourage them to think for themselves, to take the initiative, and to use their imagination. Make sure you reward them for doing so, and let them know they have the right to make mistakes now and then. Develop a good "visibility system" for keeping track of their work processes, and turn them loose. Give them elbow room to get the results, and focus your attention on results more than methods.

Practice the philosophy and the techniques of time management, and teach your staff members to do the same. Focus on results and payoffs, and they will learn to make choices maturely and effectively. As you go through a typical day, keep thinking in terms of the big picture. Keep pushing the trivia back to make room for the important. Make sure you can take a few minutes each day to sit down quietly, lean back, and reflect on your purposes and your plans. Find time now and then to think innovatively, to question your basic purposes, and to consider new ideas and new ways of doing things. Also, allow a little "cushion" of time each day, whenever possible, to handle the unforeseen events that can sometimes present you with problems. By delegating thoroughly, assigning goals and roles, planning and monitoring effectively, and managing your own time aggressively, you free yourself to accomplish the really important things. You also mobilize your staff members to work effectively in the same way. The combination of a goal-oriented, time-competent manager and a team of goal-oriented, time-competent employees makes a very effective work unit indeed.

GETTING ALONG
IN ORGANIZATIONS

UNDERSTANDING ORGANIZATIONAL POLITICS

Now we move to the next logical step in studying the area of social competence, namely the organizational level. Here, we go beyond the realm of group dynamics to consider the behavior of organizational creatures — people who deal with one another on the basis of perceived roles and programmed relationships in a hierarchical setting. This realm of study can provide some very interesting and intriguing insights into human behavior, and some practically useful ones as well.

In this chapter, we will develop some guidelines for getting what you want and going where you want to go within the domain of a typical business organization. We will briefly study organizational settings, climates, values, politics, and the kinds of skills a professional person needs to get along effectively in such a setting.

an organization
as a social system

In recent years, management theorists have shifted their attention more and more from the view of an organization, either profit making or nonprofit, as an apparatus, or *technical system,* to the view of an organization as a full-fledged miniature society, or *social system.* An effective merger of the traditional view of the technical system with the more recent view of the social system brings us to the notion of a *sociotechnical system.* In studying an organization as a sociotechnical system, we bring together topics such as human values, motivations, need-satisfactions, group behavior, social climate, structures, communication patterns, work processes, economic issues, control systems, and productivity measures, in an attempt to describe and deal with organizations in practical and realistic terms.

To navigate effectively within the social setting of a business organization requires at least a general awareness of certain characteristic features of organizational behavior, that is, the basic factors that shape the behavior of people who perceive themselves as members of an abstractly structured set of programmed relationships we call an organization.

We know, for example, that power and authority play very important roles in shaping the ways organizational people relate to one another. Every organization has a well-defined and usually well-defended hierarchy. It also has a distinctive social climate, which a fairly perceptive person can sense simply by moving around in it for a while. An organization will have certain very distinctive value systems, which regulate member behavior in various contexts and which, to a great extent, originate in the attitudes and behavior of the top managers.

Every organization has its own distinctive politics, and you as a member of the organization can only flaunt or ignore these processes at your own risk. Informal relationships that have the effect of concentrating resources around certain people, certain philosophies, and certain points of view play a crucial part in the day-to-day work life of the members. Each organization has its own particular "grapevine," or informal communication network, through which the rank-and-file members can quickly pass information of particular interest to them.

And every organization has its own top management style, the collective philosophy and behavior pattern of those in the top few seats of authority. By what these people say and do, they tend to shape the interactions of subordinate managers, their departments, and consequently the people of the organization.

By learning to assess the "lay of the land" in any particular organization and to study its more subtle human processes, you can develop a degree of versatility in dealing with others in the structured setting. You can develop what some managers call "street smarts" — the skill of getting along effectively within practical human structures that exist in the everyday business world.

the chain of command

To live and work effectively as a citizen of a sizable organization, you must understand and appreciate the significance of the *chain of command*. Every organization has one, and the managers of every organization give very careful attention to preserving it.

The term comes from ancient military theory, with the metaphor of a chain implying that there exists an unbroken line of influence from the person at the very "top" of the organization, through a succession of subordinate authority people, all the way down to the lowest ranking person at the "bottom." This concept gives a tremendous amount of theoretical reassurance to the people in the organization, satisfying their needs for structure, order, and predictability of organizational life.

To come to terms with the chain of command in an organization means realizing that every person who constitutes a "link" in the chain, that is, every manager, sees himself or herself in the context of the *management family*, and that he or she will behave according to that extremely compelling role-definition. In a sense we have only two kinds of people in the organization, management people and nonmanagement people — at least in the eyes of management people. Management people tend to feel very uncomfortable about you when you indicate by your behavior that you don't understand the chain of command, or that you don't accept and respect it.

Many women seem to have more difficulty in this respect than men, especially if they have had little exposure in their jobs to the hierarchy of the organization. They might tend to "go to the top" with a problem, determined to get action from the person they consider best placed to resolve it. In doing so, they may "violate the chain of command" by trying to go over the heads of one or more managers, who don't feel at all pleased about it. It seems that men in an organization often learn a more definite set of rules about the chain of command, possibly because men have greater access than women to the kinds of jobs that put them into contact with it.

Part of the "street smarts" you need to function effectively in the organizational setting has to do with showing that you acknowledge the chain of command and that others can trust you to work within it. This doesn't mean that you never look for alternative ways to achieve your objectives when somebody in the chain of command becomes an obstacle, or that you never resort to roundabout interpersonal strategies in the general area we call "organizational politics." It just means that you preserve the order and stability of the chain of command, and you help those who comprise it to feel comfortable about dealing with you on issues that involve authority and organizational levels.

positive politics: getting ahead with your values intact

Let's define *positive politics* as the interpersonal processes you use to get ahead in an organization while keeping your value system intact. We know that every organization has its politics. In the simplest sense, we can think of politics as simply forms of influence among people. Although the term *politics* has acquired an almost solely negative connotation these days, we can profitably use it with a neutral connotation. Let's just consider politics as something that always exists, a form of behavior in which all human beings engage, and a normal pattern by which people form coalitions and influence one another.

Sometimes a person working in an organization will say, "I don't play politics. I just do my job." Well, from the point of view of human organizational behavior, a person can't "not play." When you go to work in the organization, you automatically become part of its political processes; they won't let you out of the game. Another person might say, "You have to play politics to get ahead around here," not realizing what a true and basic statement he or she has made. The unwillingness to look at political processes realistically, and the unrealistic wish that they would disappear, obscures the logic of this person's own statement from his or her perception. *To get ahead in an organization, you must influence those who have the wherewithal to promote you.*

The person who "doesn't want to play politics" has simply adopted one particular strategy, and one of the least effective at that. He thinks that by doing his work well and not having much to do with other people, he will sooner or later get his due. He thinks that "they" *should* promote him and give him better jobs and more money simply because he does good work. Unfortunately, he doesn't realize that getting ahead requires *cooperation* with those he wants to get ahead with and get ahead of. Plain hard work usually doesn't do it. He needs an awareness of the social processes by which people come to know and respect him, and the willingness to form the positive alliances needed to gain influence and win out in competition for more attractive jobs.

Sometimes a person will say, "I got screwed by politics. They ganged up on me and killed my project, and the boss gave the funds to them for their dumb idea." Of course, the people he just described as ganging up on him wouldn't put it quite that way. "Politics had nothing to do with it," the leader might say. "I just did my homework. I had already convinced the boss to fund my project before we even went into the staff meeting." The loser calls it politics, and the winner calls it homework. I call it both, but why consider it a dirty word? One guy got what he wanted, and the other didn't. The difference lay in their strategies for influencing the decision-maker.

We can consider positive politics to consist of those actions you take to *form and service alliances* with others in the organization whose support and assistance you need in order to accomplish your objectives. It involves nothing more than honest, straightforward working relationships which you build as you go about your daily work.

Of course, if your values permit you to play really "dirty politics," then you have more options than if you prefer fair play. You can lie, cheat, steal, bribe, defame the reputations of others, and double-cross your friends freely if your values don't get in the way. For most of us, however, positive political strategies not only help us keep our value systems intact, they also work quite well in getting what we want.

We can reduce the matter of gaining organizational "clout" to a very simple principle. You, or anyone else working in an organization, will feel more willing to go along with an idea proposed by someone you like than by someone you don't like. Think about this with regard to your personal experiences. You probably tend to look for the benefits in a proposal when your friend comes up with it, and you probably feel more willing to accept some uncertainties, because you believe he or she can make it work. Your confidence in that person comes partly from having seen him or her in action in the past and partly because you simply feel attracted to him or her. You have a positive political relationship.

This all boils down to the simple political strategy of *getting people to like you* by using affirmative communication techniques as you do business with them and forming long-term alliances with those who play a key part in your objectives. If you tend toward a withdrawn, undersocial pattern of interpersonal behavior, you will find it much more difficult to get ahead politically than if you transact freely and positively with others.

Actually carrying out the strategies of positive politics may require a change in your thinking processes. You may find it necessary to give a higher priority to day-to-day relationship-building and to becoming at least casual friends with some of the people you work with in other parts of the organization. You may find that "small talk," or other casual conversations, play a significant part in getting to know another person and letting him or her get to know you. Every time you support and affirm another person, and every time you treat that person in a positive, constructive way, you create the basis for some future interaction in which you can persuade him or her to support your objectives more easily.

p.o.w.e.r.: who has it?

You don't have to deal with other people in a given organization for very long to discover the range of "clout," or interpersonal influence, they have among various hierarchical levels. We speak of a person as having power in an organization when he or she can make things happen.

We know that some people have relatively formal types of power, and others have informal types. The formal chain of command doesn't tell the whole story when it comes to total influence. For example, you may have seen an executive in a position of nominally high formal authority get pushed into a very ineffectual role by other executives. If he couldn't deploy his authority very effectively, then rank did not equate to power. You may have seen someone "promoted" to a very high level on the organization chart, as a way to "demote" him from the real power processes of the organization. A title and a fancy office constitute the "payoff" he gets for gracefully giving up his claim to real power.

You can make a quick survey of the kinds of

power people have in an organizational setting, and you can identify the high-power people, by using a simple acronym. P.O.W.E.R. equals:

Position — formal rank or entitlement to give orders.

Opportunity — a chance to take some action, or exclusive access to a means for solving an important organizational problem.

Wealth — access to or control of any organizational resource which others value and need.

Expertise — having skills or information upon which others must depend.

Relationship — having a high-quality relationship with someone who possesses Position, Opportunity, Wealth, or Expertise.

If you want to build your own influence among members of an organization, you simply have to accumulate as much of each of these power commodities as you can in the course of doing your day-to-day job. Obviously, if you go around clumsily grabbing for these forms of influence, without enabling people to see you as safely established within a nonthreatening role, you probably won't last very long. But if you build positive relationships as you go along, if you get useful and important work done, and you use the occasional natural opportunities that arise to acquire the elements of influence, you can do it quite honestly and straightforwardly. And in acquiring power, you also need to acquire the skill of handling it maturely, deftly, and gracefully.

creating your political "molecule"

If you agree that you can accomplish your ends more effectively and get ahead in your organization by forming positive alliances with others, it makes sense to decide consciously how to approach the matter. With whom will you build alliances, and how? Obviously, it makes sense to try for basically positive relationships with all of the various people you deal with in the organization. In addition, some of these relationships can play such an important part in your success that they warrant careful thought and continuing long-term "maintenance."

Take a look at the organization chart, and get a clear idea of the kinds of formal relationships that will affect you. Then diagram in any people you know who have unusually high informal power. Thinking about your promotion possibilities for jobs and roles beyond your present one, ask yourself which people will play a first-order role in your getting there. Which ones do you need to have highly positive relationships with, and which ones do you especially need to have see eye-to-eye with you on various key issues?

List the names of about eight to ten people at most whom you consider elements in your personal political "molecule." You and these other people must constitute a political unit, at least from the standpoint of cooperative relationships, common interests, and shared philosophies of life in this particular organization, and the willingness to support one another in selling new ideas and approaches. These people may reside at various levels and in various departments. They may not necessarily know that they belong to your political molecule, but you know it, and you have a definite program in mind for building and maintaining a positive relationship over the long term with each of them. Each of these people can or will play some fairly important part in your personal objectives as well as your work-related objectives.

Some of them you might see only occasionally because of their positions in the organization, while you might see others daily. Your own boss normally would belong to your political molecule. So would his or her boss. Managers and executives in other departments or other functional areas could also play a part. Make this a realistic definition, and include only those with whom you can logically expect to have first-order contact over the long term. Don't overlook relatively low-ranking people who might have a very important circumstantial effect on your objectives.

Without going out of your way, without making it obvious, and cetainly without currying favor with them, you simply have to take your time and develop with each of these people a sense of rapport and cooperative action. This positive bias will serve you well over time; it will make it easier for you to sell your ideas and approaches, and it will make them inclined to agree with you and support you more often than they disagree with you or oppose you. You can carry out this process of molecule maintenance very subtly and gracefully, keeping your own value system intact and at the same time establishing for yourself a relatively valuable "bank account" of influence with them, and consequently with others in the organization.

And when you consider the matter of your personal reputation and influence in the organization, make sure you base it on competence. Instead of trying to get ahead *only* by getting along well with others, a professional person can go further and faster by consistently getting worthwhile results and making sure those in positions of power know about it. Make sure you can do something well — something of value to the organization in the eyes of those in power. Build your political strategies upon a solid reputation for competence, and you'll have a relatively easy time practicing positive and effective politics.

managing your boss

Managing a boss means maintaining a positive working relationship with him and influencing him in such a way as to acquire sufficient running room to accomplish your work effectively and to build your own political clout in the organization.

In most cases, you can create a relatively flexible relationship with a boss by applying Albrecht's "pain-relief" theory. This theory states that a manager will tend to trust, rely on, and grant maximal autonomy to an employee whom the manager sees as connected with relief in one or more areas of "primary pain." I define a primary pain factor as any problem, issue, or requirement facing the manager which causes him a significant degree of concern. This can include virtually any aspect of the organization, the work, or the manager's individual job itself. Find out what bugs him. Any time you can take action to relieve pain for your boss, you become psychologically valuable to him. He might or might not consciously realize this, but indeed he will act upon it.

For example, you might find out that the boss frequently gets raked over the coals in the operations meeting about some particular project. You might make a habit of providing him with useful information to take along, which would help him make a stronger case for his actions and to show positive results. Since he might not think to ask you for this information, your action to relieve a primary form of pain will come as a welcome surprise.

By applying this pain-relief process consistently, methodically, and nonmanipulatively, you can become a pain-killer for your boss. By making his problems your problems, you can become, in his perception, a valuable resource, a helpful colleague, and a trustworthy professional person to whom he can grant maximal freedom of action, knowing that you will support him and make his job easier. In return, you get the political running room you need.

rules for political success

In keeping with our notion of positive politics as a matter of getting ahead with your value system intact, we can sum up some important political strategies, or policies, that will help you in virtually any organization:

1. Do something well; get recognized as an achiever.
2. Form alliances and service them regularly.
3. Get visibility.

4. Get credit for your accomplishments.
5. Relieve pain when possible.
6. Contribute to the big picture.
7. Keep developing yourself.
8. Have a plan for your progress in the organization.
9. Have options to your present job — especially in good times.
10. Know when to leave.

SPECIAL PROBLEMS
OF WOMEN
IN ORGANIZATIONS

women's mobility

Like it or not, women in organizations currently face certain subtle barriers, and some not so subtle, which make it more difficult for them than for men to move into positions with high levels of authority, high social status, and high pay. Current surveys suggest that, in the general work force, women earn an average of about two dollars per hour less than men. Women occupy fewer than one percent of all executive jobs.

Equal Employment Opportunity (EEO) legislation and litigation in the United States has certainly raised awareness of these issues. The actual effectiveness of government intervention in private sector operations remains open to debate, but at least the issues have emerged for conscious scrutiny. Some of the more obvious barriers to women's mobility no longer exist, but a number of subtle ones do indeed remain.

As an upwardly mobile woman in an organization, you need to make a realistic assessment of the particular climate in which you work, set some concrete goals, and make a plan of action. To get very far in an organization, as a general matter, you need to have as many factors working for you as possible. These include:

1. An organizational setting in which you have at least a reasonable chance of getting promoted into responsible jobs.
2. Demonstrated competence in some particular area, which managers in the organization have not stereotyped as typically "female work."
3. Some credentials you can show, such as a college degree, special training or qualifications, results from a management assessment center, or the like.
4. Demonstrated ability to grow into a challenging job; a clear self-developmental policy, and the tendency to perform capably at the level of competence associated with your next step.
5. A clear understanding of organizational politics and a well-developed set of positive relationships with key managers who can influence your career progress.
6. A serious personal commitment to a career and to getting ahead; willingness to work for long-term results.
7. Willingness to work hard and participate in the central work ethic of the organization.
8. A certain amount of psychological toughness; the ability to tolerate setbacks, inconsiderate behavior by others, and conflict without crying or otherwise becoming disabled emotionally.

None of these factors will guarantee that you will go as far in the organization or as fast as you consider reasonable. But without them, or at least a fair share of them, the odds don't look too good. Presently, an upwardly mobile woman probably needs more competence and preparation than the average man in an organization in order to go as far and as fast. Accept that as a fact of life at this particular stage. But remember, too, that men must navigate essentially the same territory as women in getting ahead, even though they have certain built-in advantages. To do well in an organization, a man must outdo a large majority of his contemporaries because, obviously, not everybody can get ahead of everybody else. A woman must outdo most of the same people that a man must outdo. Hard work, preparation, strategic thinking, and a bit of luck will work for a woman just the same as for a man.

the "ole boy" network

There exists within virtually every sizable organization an invisible "system," defined rather abstractly by certain attitudes, custom, norms, and behavior patterns, which tends to separate males and females into two distinctly different populations. Beyond the obvious gender differences, people have institutionalized various social differences which define accepted male roles and female roles. Some organizational behaviorists call this invisible system the "ole boy" network, with the connotation of the Deep South traditional view of male friendship, companionship, and mutual support. By looking at human organizational behavior from this particular point of view, you can indeed trace out the elements of such a system and see how this monolithic attitude-behavior "set" governs male-female interactions and relationships.

Females in organizations generally find themselves blocked off from certain kinds of interactions with males and from participation in certain distinctly masculine activities, which often have an important influence on the major events and processes in the organization. When males transact important kinds of organizational business within this male-only pattern of contact, they tend to exclude women automatically from the mainstream of influence. Women may or may not consciously recognize this exclusion process, but they do indeed feel its effects.

Some of the specific features of the "ole boy" syndrome include:

1. Male friendships and colleague relationships outside of work hours; men can discuss organizational matter, problems, policies, and political processes and can make various agreements for common action, without consulting female colleagues.

2. Characteristically male activities which

women do not participate in for sexually specific reasons; commonplace activities such as going to the rest room, during which time men may discuss important issues, possibly even deliberately excluding women; activities like going to a health club.

3. Traditional male entitlements or, alternatively, female prohibitions; for example, travelling on company business with other males and staying overnight automatically raises the possibility of a sexual interaction, with implications for the wives of the professional woman's colleagues; entertaining clients or visiting executives, with the tendency for males to invite females along merely for decorative or recreational purposes; males may tend to exclude females from these settings in order to avoid the ambiguity they entail.

4. Male "locker room" behavior; the relative freedom of males to use profanity, sexually oriented slang, sexually oriented jokes, double-meaning remarks, and similar forms of humor, and analogies between male sexual functions and business activities; the tendency to subtly remind a lone woman in an otherwise all-male group of her status as a sexual object, even by paradoxically deferring to her status and "keeping it clean"; social traditions which prevent women from using sexually oriented language.

5. Traditional disparities between male language habits and female language habits; men tend to use figures of speech that suggest strong, aggressive, or dominating action, while women tend to use softer forms which emphasize accommodation, feelings, and values; tendency of many women to over-use qualifiers and superlatives in their speech, thereby diminishing its forcefulness; tendency of men to use analogies and metaphors of sport and warfare, for example, "game plan," "who has the ball," and "lead the charge," while women tend to shy away from these constructions; tendency of men and women both to refer to women in the organization as "girls."

It makes little sense for an upwardly mobile woman to try to fight the "ole boy" syndrome head-on, or to try to change such a deeply ingrained conceptual structure. It makes more sense to avoid confrontations with this invisible system and to take your lumps gracefully when it does happen. As later sections show, you can still meet your major objectives if the organization has at least a reasonably humane atmosphere of male-female relationships.

the "ole girl" network

Many upwardly mobile women don't realize it, but there also exists in any sizable organization a parallel social structure to the "ole boy" network, namely, the "ole girl" network. Just as you have to look at the work patterns in a certain way to discern the male-oriented invisible system, so too you have to observe female work behavior carefully to see the alternative system. You can trace out the "ole girl" network in terms of some of the following processes:

1. Female-stereotyped jobs; managers and personnel people in most organizations have fairly distinct attitudes about which jobs to put women into and which jobs to put men into; women and men themselves tend to perceive these stereotypes unconsciously, and they automatically tend to act in ways that reinforce them.

2. Preoccupation of many women, in talking casually to one another, with typically "girl" issues, for example, houses, husbands, babies, clothes, cooking, personal relationships, and who sleeps with whom in the organization.

3. "Derived status" among women who work as secretaries to managers at various levels; the "executive secretary syndrome," in which an executive's secretary uses informal aspects of her position to gain influence over the other women.

4. Anthropological tendencies of women to compete with one another for favored status with the dominant male in a group, that is, the male boss; lack of a strong teamwork ethic among women in dealing with organizational matters; tendency toward backstabbing and personal attack, rather than doing battle over concrete issues.

5. Using sexuality, either subtly or overtly, to manipulate men in positions of influence in order to gain in status among women or to serve personal ends; choosing to "butter up" influential men, flirt with them, or actually grant sexual favors to them, rather than deal with them assertively as mature professional people.

Like it or not, the tendency of a large majority of women in a typical organization to approach their jobs as women — or "girls" — first, and as professonal working people second, creates a distinct separation between working men and working women. Notwithstanding the current attention given to women's mobility, the majority of working women still seem to place home and husband highest on their list of values, and most still see "working" as a necessary evil — a holding pattern they have to stay in until they get married, or, if married, a way to bring in enough money to enjoy the American "good life." As more and more women decide to place their careers first in their lives, or at least on an equal par with their husbands, the "ole girl" syndrome will probably continue to weaken and lose its monolithic influence. But at present, let's not declare it dead just because we want it to die.

Unfortunately, the existence of the "ole girl" syndrome confronts many upwardly mobile women with an unearned credibility gap in dealing with males in the organization, and in declaring themselves as serious contenders for positions of responsibility. To make matters worse, those women who choose to stay "girls" and to play by the "ole girl" network's rules will often try to undermine the progress of those who try to opt out of it, by back-stabbing, character assassination, and poisoning the attitudes of key males by manipulative means. Since women in general don't seem to adhere to the team ethic as much as men do, and they don't seem to recognize the legitimacy of any "Marquis of Queensbury" rules for interpersonal relations, the upwardly mobile woman sometimes finds her greatest source of difficulty in the reactions of the "ole girls" as she begins to outgrow them and outpace them.

some useful strategies
for upwardly mobile women

In addition to acquiring and using the various competencies of personal effectiveness we've explored in this book, it helps to have a few conscious strategies for maximizing your progress in the organization. Keep at least the following factors in mind:

1. Resign your membership in the "ole girl" club; you can't play in two leagues at the same time; keep as many of your friendships as possible, but don't let other women drag you into their games — the men with whom you must deal will never take you seriously or feel safe in working with you if you don't make the transition from the "ole girl" to the "new professional woman"; don't use your sexuality to get your way one day and expect them to treat you as a colleague the next.

2. Declare yourself; have an interview with your boss, and let him or her know politely but definitely that you intend to carve out a career for yourself, and that you want his or her help and support; ask the boss to acknowledge your right to meaningful work and peer status with men doing the same kinds of work and to agree to encourage male members of the work unit to stop assuming that you should automatically do female-stereotyped jobs like taking notes at the staff meeting (unless your job definition involves that); go to the personnel officer and enlist his or her help in making a career plan and in making it known in the organization that you intend to go for a career; go to the training officer and sign up for company-provided management training if you want to move in that direction, or if none exists, ask for company reimbursement for evening study; collect the various records of your completed training and make sure they go into your personnel file.

3. Use time to your advantage; learn, de-

velop, and educate yourself; have a long-term view as well as short-term tactics.

4. Get a mentor; try to interest someone in an influential management position in advising you, guiding you, helping you develop, and helping you get visibility to higher management; avoid a sexual connection in this area, at all costs.

5. Study, understand, and respect the chain of command.

6. Teach yourself not to cry when you get angry; instead of directing your anger inward at yourself and becoming tearful or depressed at setbacks, direct it outward in definite, result-producing ways; never do battle on the personal level — keep your confrontations centered on meaningful business issues.

7. Learn to handle male condescension without getting disabled; don't signal-react to terms like "girl," "women's lib," or the various sugary put-downs men use in trying to push women into subordinate status; learn to preserve your self-esteem, and you won't react either defensively or aggressively.

8. Don't squander your energies on "causes"; make your career your primary cause; don't get tangled in women's crusades and battles for social justice that only ventilate anger and undermine your reputation with the men with whom you must come to terms; support general organizational programs for women, but make it plain that you don't depend on a general solution to the problem of women's rights in order to get where you want to go.

9. Form a support system with other women in the organization; trade information, scuttlebutt, ideas, and strategies; help one another, and above all learn to take joint action instead of undermining one another.

10. Get your name on paper; establish name recognition by putting your own name on as many of the memos, reports, and letters that you write as possible; let people know you exist and that you play a noticeable part in the day-to-day affairs of the organization.

11. Don't fake it; don't pretend to know what you don't know and don't try to one-up people; build on solid competence and accomplishment.

12. Don't overdo the "image" routine; take the "dress for success" books and other show-business tactics with a grain of salt; "formula" people stick out like a sore thumb; adopt an attractive, comfortable, businesslike style that you like and that suits you; don't come on too strong and bowl others over with the self-consciously assertive style many women use to undermine their own interpersonal effectiveness.

13. Don't sacrifice your humanity to get ahead; keep your values intact and your soul your own.

MANAGING
YOUR CAREER

Recalling the concept of a balanced life-style, which we studied in Chapter 7, and considering your career as simply one important element in a total package of activities that make your life enjoyable, you can adopt some conscious and fairly systematic policies for managing your career. You can maximize career advancement and enjoyment while fitting your work into the overall perspective of a balanced life-style.

avoiding the dead end

First, of course, comes the conscious policy of looking ahead in your career. In addition to enjoying your work on a short-term basis, you need to keep moving in a productive and promising direction, and especially to avoid the career "dead-end" situation. In practical terms, you've arrived at a dead end when you no longer like your job *and* you have no really attractive options at the moment — either in the same organization or outside. For example, you may have reached the end of a short career "ladder" with your present organization, or you may have run out of satisfying work to do there, or you may have lost interest in your field of specialty, or you may have gotten yourself into a political jam with somebody higher up in the management hierarchy. For these or any of a number of other reasons, you might want out, but you might not have an attractive out to take.

Rather than dealing with an immediate dead-end situation, you need to avoid getting into one. A general review of your circumstances from time to time can help here. By making a critical examination of your overall career field, then looking at your present organization, and then evaluating your current assignment, you can make a conscious assessment and decide whether the time has come for a major change. You've probably already assessed your salary, fringe benefits, and the nonmonetary pros and cons of your present situation. Keep in mind, too, the tremendous importance over the long run of having satisfying work to do. Too many people live out unpleasant and unfulfilling work lives because they really haven't appreciated the importance and the possibilities of finding satisfying work. If you've reached the point where you say "It's just a job," then you've dead-ended and the time has come for a major change.

You might want to define or redefine your career for any number of reasons, or at any number of possible junctures in your life. You might have just started out in the work world or in a new career field. Or, you might have reached a midcareer point and feel the need for some significant stage of self-renewal. You might have completed one career, and instead of deciding to "retire," you might want to

202

start a brand new career, under different circumstances. Or, like so many people, you may have grown tired of the constraints of organizational living, and you might want to "do your own thing," striking out on your own somehow. Whatever the case, some careful and logical thinking seems appropriate. The practical action techniques of getting organized and of solving problems and making decisions will also apply especially well here.

You need to define a fairly specific sense of thrust for your career, and for the next half-year and the next few years. Where do you want to go? What new territory do you want to explore? What new experiences and competencies do you want to acquire? You might find it helpful to attend a career-planning workshop to get some useful ideas and techniques.

Once you've established a general aiming point, you need to put together a concrete, specific, practical, and realistic plan for getting there. You have to account for all the major action you'll have to take, the major adjustments you'll have to make, and the costs of doing it all. Lay out the plan and get started.

career strategies and policies

You may find it helpful to adopt some definite policies about the kinds of job situations you will accept and the kinds of opportunities you will pursue. This helps in making choices, especially when you find yourself entertaining a variety of disparate options. By knowing fairly specifically what you want and what you don't want, you can make the choices more effectively. You can also develop new options to suit your interests.

In setting career policies, you can consider at least the following areas:

1. The general fields you will and won't consider; specific areas of work within your field.
2. Specific features of the work, for example, dealing with people, travel, and so on.
3. Organizational setting — big organization, small one, self-employed.
4. Profit-making organization vs. nonprofit, government, social service, and so on.
5. Formal education, and the part it will play in your career.
6. Mobility — geographic locations you will consider living and working in.
7. Specialist-type work or generalist.

8. Managerial/administrative or strictly technical.

9. Earnings you consider essential.

10. Pressure, pace, and stress you will accept as part of the job situation.

Think through each of these areas very carefully. You might decide to suspend judgement on some of them until you've had a chance to explore some of the options available and to consider some of the pros and cons. Just make sure you keep the decision issue in sight, and resolve it within a reasonable length of time. Once you've made some fairly firm decisions in each of the above policy categories, and any other particular categories you've added to the list, write your policies down. Put them in the form of simple statements, preferably on a single sheet of paper. Keep it handy and review it occasionally.

knowing when to bail out

There may come a time in your organizational life when you need to make a swift exit, preferably gracefully, but possibly ungracefully. Most commonly, a person gets into a political jam and can't find a satisfactory resolution. You might find that, despite your best efforts, someone in a position above you in the organization takes a dislike to you, considers you a threat to his or her security, or simply finds you and your activities distasteful, unattractive, threatening, or otherwise undesirable. Don't expect everyone in a management position to have a high degree of maturity, or to believe enthusiastically in fair play. You may look up one day and see the handwriting on the wall. He or she may have begun sharpening the knife for your precious bones. Unless you want to make a sporty course of it and try to topple that person from power, it makes sense to "get while the gettin's good."

If at all possible, *leave of your own volition,* in an atmosphere of parting amicably with the organization. Minimize the significance of the conflict with the other person, rely on your existing political relationships to cast you in a positive light, and don't burn any bridges. In all likelihood, the person upstairs will find this a satisfactory resolution, since, after all, he or she really only wants you gone rather than dead. You save face for yourself by saving face for the other person. In any case, your colleagues who remain will probably spread the word subtly that the person upstairs unfairly forced you out of the organization and that they've lost a valued associate. You live to fight another day.

As the old expression goes, as they run you out of town, grab a flag and wave it. Make it look like a parade, with you out in front leading it.

keeping your options open

Think of the satisfaction you'd feel in the following situation. You've gotten into an irresolvable political jam with someone upstairs in the organization, and it looks terminal. Your friends and colleagues recognize you as a marked person. It simply resolves to a question of how and when the other person will get you.

One day you walk into work, whistling cheerfully, and you announce graciously to your boss that, much as you regret leaving, you've received an incredibly attractive job offer with another organization and you've reluctantly decided to leave for much greener pastures. Within two to three weeks, you've departed the winner and left behind an inspiring memory for others who might find themselves in the same fix.

Did you just happen to stumble into the new opportunity within a week or two after you saw the handwriting on the wall? Not likely. This could only happen, in real life, if you had planned ahead — if you had prepared for the eventuality even *before* it ever developed. By having a conscious "options policy," you managed to make a graceful exit, and even to gain ground.

Having an options policy means quietly staying in circulation in the job market for your particular field, checking now and then to see what other possibilities may exist and occasionally entertaining an offer from another organization. Although very few people realize it, a politically conscious, career-minded professional needs to have options *in good times*, just as much as in hard times. Trying to come up with an attractive job alternative within a few weeks, after you start to feel the hot breath on the back of your neck, seldom works out well. Most people react to good times, that is, a satisfying job, by settling down, getting comfortable, dropping all their connections to the outside job market, and enjoying life. But the tables can turn on you amazingly fast. You can go from the fair-haired person one day to the sacrificial lamb the next, and maybe not even know how or why.

By continually keeping a few attractive options open, you can react quickly and gracefully to a sudden political reversal in the organization. In this way, if you want to leave, you don't have to start from scratch, or with a defensive, one-down attitude. You may not always have the ideal alternative in hand, but having one or more reasonably attractive ones works so much better than suddenly finding yourself thrust into the search mode.

Few professional people realize the significance of this options policy to their careers. Those who have tried it, however, and found that it saved their hides in one or more very uncomfortable situations, become permanent believers.

INDEX